Grammar, Usage, and Mechanics Book

McDougal Littell

GRADE EIGHT

Teaching

More Practice

Application

McDougal Littell
A HOUGHTON MIFFLIN COMPANY
Evanston, Illinois Boston Dallas

ISBN-13: 978-0-618-15382-4 ISBN-10: 0-618-15382-9

19 20 21 DSHV 11 10 09

Contents

Special Features

The *Grammar, Usage, and Mechanics Copymasters/Workbook* contains a wealth of skill-building exercises.

Each lesson has different levels of worksheets. **Teaching** introduces the skill; **More Practice** and **Application** extend the skill with advanced exercises.

Each page focuses on one topic or skill. A brief instructional summary on the **Teaching** page is followed by reinforcement activities.

Key words and phrases are highlighted for greater clarity and ease of use.

When appropriate, example sentences demonstrate how to complete exercises.

Tabs make it easy to navigate the book.

Name ______________________ Date ______

Lesson 1

Complete Subjects and Predicates

Teaching

CHAPTER 1

A **sentence** is a group of words that expresses a complete thought. Every complete sentence has two basic parts: a subject and a predicate.

The **complete subject** includes all the words that tell whom or what the sentence is about.

The rays of the sun give energy to the earth.

The **complete predicate** includes the verb and all the words that tell what the subject is or what the subject does.

Energy is needed for work.

Identifying Complete Subjects and Complete Predicates

Underline the complete subject once and the complete predicate twice.

Example The energy in food makes our muscles work.

1. People of long ago used animals as a source of energy.
2. Strong animals plowed fields for farmers.
3. Coal, oil, and natural gas are called fossil fuels.
4. Fossil fuels come from the remains of prehistoric plants and animals.
5. The earth contains a limited supply of fossil fuels.
6. Modern humans use fossil fuels more than any other type of energy.
7. Energy from the sun is stored in oil, wood, and coal.
8. Waterfalls or rapids produce energy.
9. Many early cotton mills were built near waterfalls.
10. The energy of the water ran the machinery in the factory.
11. Inventors introduced the steam engine.
12. Hydroelectric plants now make use of water energy in rivers and waterfalls.
13. Many appliances need electrical energy to work.
14. Electricity is necessary for the modern way of life.
15. Wind energy turns windmills.
16. The energy of the wind also moves boats with sails.
17. Solar furnaces collect the sun's rays with mirrors.
18. Solar energy cells can heat a home even in winter.
19. The gasoline engine produces energy for our cars.
20. Nuclear power plants change nuclear energy into electrical energy.
21. All these kinds of energy are important to life on Earth.

Grammar, Usage, and Mechanics Book 1

Name ______________________________ Date ______________

Lesson 1

Complete Subjects and Predicates

Teaching

CHAPTER 1

A **sentence** is a group of words that expresses a complete thought. Every complete sentence has two basic parts: a subject and a predicate.

The **complete subject** includes all the words that tell whom or what the sentence is about.

The rays of the sun give energy to the earth.

The **complete predicate** includes the verb and all the words that tell what the subject is or what the subject does.

Energy is needed for work.

Identifying Complete Subjects and Complete Predicates

Underline the complete subject once and the complete predicate twice.

EXAMPLE The energy in food makes our muscles work.

1. People of long ago used animals as a source of energy.
2. Strong animals plowed fields for farmers.
3. Coal, oil, and natural gas are called fossil fuels.
4. Fossil fuels come from the remains of prehistoric plants and animals.
5. The earth contains a limited supply of fossil fuels.
6. Modern humans use fossil fuels more than any other type of energy.
7. Energy from the sun is stored in oil, wood, and coal.
8. Waterfalls or rapids produce energy.
9. Many early cotton mills were built near waterfalls.
10. The energy of the water ran the machinery in the factory.
11. Inventors introduced the steam engine.
12. Hydroelectric plants now make use of water energy in rivers and waterfalls.
13. Many appliances need electrical energy to work.
14. Electricity is necessary for the modern way of life.
15. Wind energy turns windmills.
16. The energy of the wind also moves boats with sails.
17. Solar furnaces collect the sun's rays with mirrors.
18. Solar energy cells can heat a home even in winter.
19. The gasoline engine produces energy for our cars.
20. Nuclear power plants change nuclear energy into electrical energy.
21. All these kinds of energy are important to life on Earth.

Name ______________________________ Date ______________

Lesson 1

Complete Subjects and Predicates

More Practice

CHAPTER 1

A. Identifying Complete Subjects and Predicates

Draw a vertical line between the complete subject and the complete predicate in each of the following sentences.

EXAMPLE Water power | is an important energy source.

1. Petroleum is the most widely used fossil fuel.
2. The production of electricity and steel requires a large amount of coal.
3. The cleanest fossil fuel is natural gas.
4. Natural gas heats many homes and factories.
5. Solar cells convert the light of the sun into energy.
6. A strong and steady wind is necessary for successful conversion of wind power into energy.
7. Tidal power produces a very small amount of energy.
8. The battery-like fuel cell makes electricity chemically.
9. Some cities get electricity by burning trash.
10. Scientists and engineers are developing better sources of energy for the future.

B. Using Complete Subjects and Predicates

On the line to the right of each item, write how each group of words could be used: **CS** for a complete subject or **CP** for a complete predicate. Then use each group of words in a complete sentence, adding a complete subject or complete predicate as needed.

EXAMPLE bright sunlight *CS*
Bright sunlight streamed through my window this morning.

1. a strong wind

____

2. floated down the river

____

3. electric cars

____

4. wrote a report

____

Name ______________________ Date ____________

Lesson 1

Complete Subjects and Predicates

Application

A. Revising by Adding Details

Add details to the subjects and predicates to make more interesting sentences.

1. Wind blows.

____

2. Machines work.

____

3. Electricity flows.

____

4. Windmills turn.

____

5. The sun shines.

____

6. Cars need.

____

B. Writing with Complete Subjects and Complete Predicates

Imagine that you have taken these notes for a report. As you review your notes, you will rewrite fragments as complete sentences. Write the following notes as sentences that have complete subjects and predicates. If you like, you may combine two or more fragments in a single sentence.

Geothermal power. Produced when water comes into contact with heated rocks under the earth. Steam trapped underground. Power companies drill into steam. Steam turns turbines. Produces electricity. Advantage—no pollution. Cheap source of electricity. Geothermal plants in Italy, Japan, Philippines, U.S. Not a main source of energy today. Could be in the future.

____

____

____

____

____

____

____

____

Name ______________________________ Date ______________

Lesson 2

Simple Subjects

Teaching

CHAPTER 1

The **simple subject** is the main word or words in the complete subject. Words that describe the subject are not part of the simple subject. In the following sentences, the simple subjects are underlined.

Athletes all over the world enjoy extreme sports.
COMPLETE SUBJECT — COMPLETE PREDICATE

If a proper name is used as the subject, all parts of the name make up the simple subject.

Dr. Evans at the sports clinic treats many sports injuries.
COMPLETE SUBJECT — COMPLETE PREDICATE

Identifying Simple Subjects

Underline the simple subject in each sentence.

1. Extreme sports are a new kind of entertainment.
2. Participants in these sports sometimes ignore the danger.
3. The athletes enjoy the great challenge in each sport.
4. Great skill is needed for mountain biking.
5. The rider travels down a high hill or mountain on a narrow track.
6. A cross-country biker follows a rough course over a long distance.
7. The position of the rider's body is very important in mountain biking.
8. Only brave swimmers use surfboards in giant waves.
9. A new extreme sport is body surfing.
10. The body surfer rides the waves without a board.
11. Both arms of the body surfer must be extended in front.
12. The feet must be together.
13. Body surfers on a wave dive underwater as they get close to the beach.
14. Another popular ocean sport is body boarding.
15. Regular surfers stand on their surfboards.
16. Body boarders lie down on their stomachs.
17. Some athletes do spinners and El Rollos on their body boards.
18. Another extreme sport is skydiving.
19. Several sites on the Internet give information about extreme sports.
20. Sports equipment is also advertised.

Name ________________________________ Date ______________

Lesson 2

Simple Subjects

More Practice

CHAPTER 1

A. Identifying Simple Subjects

Underline the simple subject in each of the following sentences.

1. The sport of wakeboarding is becoming very popular.
2. The water-skier uses a large board instead of water skis.
3. A powerful boat pulls the wakeboarder across the water.
4. The wakeboarder makes the board do whole and half turns in the water or in the air.
5. Some people consider off-road in-line skating another extreme sport.
6. Great endurance is needed when skating on a beach or over rough ground.
7. Another new sport is snowboarding.
8. The rider of a snowboard stands sideways on the board.
9. An extreme snowboarder goes from the top of a mountain to the bottom using only the snowboard.
10. Falls are very common in this sport.

B. Writing Simple Subjects

Choose one of the following simple subjects to complete each sentence below.

athletes	Cavers	Parachutists	mountaineer
bikes	rafts	stunts	Snowboarders

1. A ____________________ is a person who climbs the tallest mountains of the world.
2. ____________________ explore deep underground caverns.
3. White-water ____________________ must be made of tough material.
4. ____________________ sometimes choose to jump off high mountains.
5. Mountain ____________________ must be made strong for riding over rough roads.
6. ____________________ use special bindings to keep their feet from slipping off the board.
7. Dangerous ____________________ can cause serious injuries.
8. Well-trained ____________________ must work out constantly to keep in shape.

Name ______________________________ Date ______________

Lesson 2

Simple Subjects

Application

CHAPTER 1

A. Writing Simple Subjects in Sentences

Use each of these words as the simple subject in a sentence.

1. danger ______________________________

____

2. climbers ______________________________

____

3. athletes ______________________________

____

4. reporters ______________________________

____

5. safety ______________________________

____

6. excitement ______________________________

____

B. Revising

Read this paragraph carefully. In some sentences, the writer has left out some of the simple subjects. When you find a sentence without a simple subject, insert this proofreading symbol ^ and write a simple subject in the space above it.

EXAMPLE Extreme ^sports^ are not for everyone.

TV has made extreme sports very popular. Now can watch athletes try seemingly impossible stunts. One new sport is called skysurfing. The wears a regular parachute. A specially designed board is strapped to the feet. The jumps out of the plane when it reaches the proper altitude. The is not open yet, so the skysurfer is freefalling through the air at 120 miles per hour. The is moved with the feet so the athlete can perform spins and flips. Finally the opens. The surfer floats safely to the ground.

Name ______________________________ Date ______________

Lesson 3

Simple Predicates, or Verbs

Teaching

CHAPTER 1

The **simple predicate,** or **verb,** is the main word or words in the complete predicate. In the following sentence, the simple predicate, or verb, is underlined.

Many unusual plants <u>grow</u> in the rain forest. (*grow in the rain forest* is the complete predicate)

VERB

The verb can be a single word as in the sentence above, or a **verb phrase,** as in the sentence below.

Exotic animals <u>can be found</u> there.

VERB PHRASE

Verbs are words used to express actions, conditions, or states of being. **Linking verbs** tell what the subject is. **Action verbs** tell what the subject does, even when the action cannot be seen.

Identifying Simple Predicates, or Verbs

Underline the simple predicate, or verb, in each sentence.

1. Most of the rain forests grow near the equator.
2. The temperature in the rain forest remains hot all year long.
3. Rain falls nearly every day in some part of the forest.
4. Humid air makes the rain forest uncomfortable for most people.
5. More types of trees grow in the rain forest than anywhere else on earth.
6. Some trees reach 200 feet in height.
7. The trees block the sunlight from the floor of the forest.
8. People walk through the forest with little trouble.
9. Some rain forests contain a jungle.
10. A jungle forms in certain sunny areas of the forest.
11. Dense plant growth makes travel through the jungle difficult.
12. Rain forests harbor about half of all the species of plants in the world.
13. Flowering plants bloom all year long.
14. Air plants thrive on the branches of trees.
15. Ferns and orchids are two kinds of air plants.
16. Other plants twine around the branches and trunks of trees.
17. Many different kinds of birds and reptiles live in the forest.
18. Colorful parrots eat fruits and nuts from the trees.
19. Monkeys swing from tree to tree.
20. Lizards and snakes slither among the branches.

Name ______________________________ Date ______________

Lesson 3

Simple Predicates, or Verbs

More Practice

A. Identifying Simple Predicates, or Verbs

Underline the simple predicate, or verb, in each of the following sentences.

1. The Amazon rain forest is the biggest in the world.
2. Other rain forests grow in Africa, Asia, and islands in the Pacific Ocean.
3. All rain forests stay green throughout the year.
4. Thundershowers soak the rain forest frequently.
5. The tops of the tallest trees form an upper canopy over the forest.
6. Slightly shorter trees make a lower canopy high above the forest floor.
7. Some animals live their entire lives between the upper and lower canopy.
8. They never descend to the ground.
9. Sloths feed on the abundant leaves in the canopy.
10. Anteaters and opossums hang by their tails from the tree branches.

B. Writing Simple Predicates, or Verbs

Choose one of the following simple predicates, or verbs, to complete each sentence below.

live	roam	fly	build	sip
hop	study	contain	eat	grow

1. Colorful toucans ______________ from branch to branch in the rain forest.
2. Hummingbirds ______________ nectar from the flowering trees.
3. Several kinds of frogs ______________ from branch to branch.
4. Deer, hogs, and other animals ______________ through the forest.
5. They ______________ roots, seeds, leaves, and fruit.
6. Termites ______________ huge colonies.
7. Different nuts and fruits ______________ on the many trees.
8. Parts of some plants ______________ special medicines.
9. Scientists ______________ the many plants and animals in the rain forest.
10. A few native people ______________ in small villages in the forest.

CHAPTER 1

Name ______________________________ Date ______________

Lesson 3

Simple Predicates, or Verbs

Application

A. Writing Simple Predicates, or Verbs, in Sentences

Use each of these words as the simple predicate, or verb, in a sentence.

1. spread ______________________________

____

2. shelter ______________________________

____

3. give ______________________________

____

4. make ______________________________

____

5. save ______________________________

____

CHAPTER 1

B. Revising

Read this paragraph carefully. In some sentences, the writer has left out the simple predicates, or verbs. When you find a sentence without a simple predicate, or verb, insert this proofreading symbol ^ and write a verb in the space above it.

Example Rain forests ^serve as a precious natural resource.

Rain forests places of great natural beauty. They contain more species of plants and animals than any other forests in the world. Many plants rare and valuable. Some animals in one particular rain forest and nowhere else. In the past, few people lived in the forest. Most visitors just to study the plants and animals. Today, more people want the products of the forest. They valuable trees, such as mahogany and rosewood. They capture some of the rare animals and reptiles. Others claim the land itself. They the rain forest for their farms and ranches. Miners for valuable minerals. Many people fear for the unique plants and animals of the rain forest.

Name ______________________ Date ______________

Lesson 4

Verb Phrases

Teaching

CHAPTER 1

The simple predicate, or verb, may consist of two or more words. These words are called the **verb phrase.** A verb phrase is made up of a main verb and one or more helping verbs.

A **main verb** can stand by itself as the simple predicate of a sentence.

The human brain directs our bodies.
MAIN VERB (ACTION)

Our brain is very important.
MAIN VERB (LINKING)

Helping verbs help the main verb express action or show time.

The brain could be called the body's control center. (*could be* is the helping verb; *called* is the main verb)

Common Helping Verbs	
Forms of be	is, am, are, was, were, be, been
Forms of do	do, does, did
Forms of have	has, have, had
Others	may, might, can, could, will, would, shall, should

Identifying Verb Phrases

Underline the verb phrase in each sentence. Include main verbs and helping verbs.

1. The human brain is receiving messages all the time.
2. Some messages are telling the brain about conditions in the body.
3. Our senses will send messages about the world around us.
4. The brain can process the messages very quickly.
5. It can guide the body's reactions in an instant.
6. Our brain could be compared to a library, a storage area of information.
7. Even our thoughts and emotions are coming from the brain.
8. No other animals' brains have developed as highly as human brains.
9. I can do many activities impossible for other animals.
10. What other animal can write a song or a poem?
11. Do you know the three main parts of the brain?
12. The cerebrum has been studied by many scientists.
13. Damage to the cerebellum might cause a problem with balance.
14. Certain body functions are controlled by the brain stem.
15. Special x-ray machines may teach us more about the brain.
16. Some brain diseases have been discovered with these machines.

Name ______________________________ Date ______________

Lesson 4

Verb Phrases

More Practice

A. Identifying Main Verbs and Helping Verbs

Underline the main verb once and the helping verb twice in each of the following sentences.

EXAMPLE Scientists are learning new information about the brain.

1. The human brain is studied by many kinds of scientists.
2. Some have been looking at the chemicals in the brain.
3. The wrong balance of chemicals could change our thoughts or actions.
4. Other scientists are learning about diseases of the brain.
5. They might study brain waves with special instruments.
6. Powerful machines can take detailed pictures of the brain.
7. Doctors may try new medicines for certain diseases.
8. Some researchers are studying processes of thought and memory.
9. Exactly how does the brain work?
10. We may know the answer to that question in the future.

B. Writing Verb Phrases

Add a helping verb to complete the verb phrase in each sentence below.

1. ______________ you understand the thought patterns of animals?
2. Scientists ______________ been doing studies on animal brains.
3. For a long time they ______________ known that the brains of other animals are more simple than human ones.
4. They ______________ know for sure that worms and insects have groups of nerve cells.
5. These animals ______________ gather information from their senses.
6. They ______________ react to things but cannot think.
7. The brains of sharks and other fish ______________ remained rather simple over time.
8. These animals ______________ listed far below squirrels in brain power.
9. The chimpanzee's brain ______________ be classified as most like the human brain.
10. No one ______________ discovered an organ as complex as the human brain.

CHAPTER 1

Name ______________________ Date ______________

Lesson 4

Verb Phrases

Application

A. Writing Sentences Using Verb Phrases

Make a verb phrase by adding a helping verb to each main verb below. Then write a sentence using the verb phrase. Underline the verb phrase.

CHAPTER 1

EXAMPLE collect
The brain can collect information rapidly.

1. think

____

2. feel

____

3. read

____

4. remember

____

5. react

____

6. sleep

____

B. Writing Using Verb Phrases

Use at least four of the following verb phrases in a story. Write the story on the lines below and underline the verb phrases that you have used. If you like, you can change the tense of the verbs in your paragraph.

is thinking	did stop	will discover	could be compared
should use	are working	can take	have been made

____

____

____

____

____

____

____

____

Name ____ Date ________________

Lesson 5

Compound Sentence Parts

Teaching

A **compound subject** is made up of two or more subjects that share the same verb. The subjects are joined by a conjunction, or connecting word, such as *and, or,* or *but.*

Dogs and cats are the most common household pets.
COMPOUND SUBJECT — PREDICATE

A **compound verb** is made up of two or more verbs that share the same subject. The verbs are joined by a conjunction such as *and, or,* or *but.*

Unusual pets demand and receive more care.
SUBJECT — COMPOUND VERB

CHAPTER 1

Identifying Compound Sentence Parts

In each sentence, underline the words in the compound subject or the compound verb. Do not underline the conjunctions that join the words. On the line to the right, write **CS** for compound subject or **CV** for compound verb.

1. Canaries and parakeets are popular pets. ______
2. Some canaries sing and chirp merrily all day long. ______
3. Parakeets say and repeat words and sounds. ______
4. Tropical fish and goldfish are also common pets. ______
5. Fancy aquariums or plain glass bowls are in many homes. ______
6. Lively fish dart and hide among the rocks and seaweed on the bottom of the tank. ______
7. Hamsters or guinea pigs make good pets for people who live in a city. ______
8. These animals mainly eat and play in small cages. ______
9. Proper food and water are necessary for all pets. ______
10. Many pets enjoy and appreciate special treats occasionally. ______
11. In the country, some children raise and train different farm animals. ______
12. Horses and goats may become their pets. ______
13. Sometimes, rabbits or chickens are raised as pets. ______
14. Any pet grows and thrives in a caring home. ______
15. Neither wild animals nor exotic reptiles should be kept as pets. ______
16. Some untamed animals chew or rip furniture. ______
17. Others carry and spread unusual diseases among the family. ______
18. Loyal pets and caring owners make the best combination of all. ______

Name ______________________ Date ______________

Lesson 5

Compound Sentence Parts

More Practice

CHAPTER 1

A. Identifying Subjects and Verbs

In the following sentences underline the subjects once and the verbs twice.

Example My dog chases and returns a thrown stick.

1. Jamie washes and brushes his Irish setter often.
2. Jamie's dog and his cat are good friends, most of the time.
3. The veterinarian checks and inoculates the pets as needed.
4. Jamie's family buys and serves healthy foods to the pets.
5. The loyal setter loves and protects Jamie in return.
6. The cat and her kittens keep life busy and entertaining.

B. Using Compound Subjects and Compound Verbs

Combine the sentence pairs to form a new sentence with the sentence part in parentheses. Use the conjunction—*and, or, nor,* or *but*—that makes the most sense.

Example The fish in my aquarium swim all day. They eat all day. (compound verb)
The fish in my aquarium swim and eat all day.

1. Gerbils exercise on a small wheel. Hamsters exercise on a wheel too. (compound subject)

 ____

2. The hamster's cage should be cleaned often. It should be scrubbed, as well. (compound verb)

 ____

3. Sometimes my cat purrs when I come home. Other times when I come home, she meows. (compound verb)

 ____

4. Cats enjoy playing with balls of yarn. Kittens also enjoy playing with balls of yarn. (compound subject)

 ____

5. Faithful dogs are good companions for many people. Faithful cats are good companions for many people, too.

 ____

Name ______________________ Date ______________

Lesson 5

Compound Sentence Parts

Application

A. Sentence Combining with Compound Subjects and Compound Verbs

Write sentences using these compound subjects and compound verbs.

1. barks or growls

____

2. parakeets and canaries

____

3. feed and water

____

4. mice and gerbils

____

5. watch and protect

____

B. More Sentence Combining

Revise the following paragraph, using compound subjects and compound verbs to combine sentences with similar ideas. Write the new paragraph on the lines below. You may need to change some verbs to make the verbs agree with the compound subjects.

You can teach many animals to do tricks. Dogs will roll over for a treat. They will beg for one too. Cats can learn very simple tricks. Birds can learn very simple tricks as well. As a trainer, your job is simple but time-consuming. You show the pet what to do. You tell the pet what to do. You repeat the process many times. Your pet repeats the process over and over as well. When your pet does the trick correctly, praise your pet. Also reward the pet. Treats make good rewards for a job well done. Pats are a good reward, also. Remember that tricks can be difficult for your pet. Patience is needed to teach a pet good tricks. Hard work is needed to teach a pet, too.

____

____

____

____

____

____

____

Name ______________________________ Date ______________

Lesson 6

Kinds of Sentences

Teaching

A **declarative sentence** expresses a statement. It ends with a period.

> **A successful inventor must use both knowledge and creativity.**

An **interrogative sentence** asks a question. It ends with a question mark.

> **Who invented the telephone?**

An **imperative sentence** tells or asks someone to do something. It usually ends with a period but may end with an exclamation point.

> **Name the inventor of the telegraph. Answer the question and win $1,000!**

An **exclamatory sentence** shows strong feeling. It always ends with an exclamation point.

> **I'm so glad someone invented the computer!**

Identifying Kinds of Sentences

On the line, identify each sentence below by writing **D** for declarative, **INT** for interrogative, **IMP** for imperative, or **E** for exclamatory. Add the proper punctuation mark at the end of each sentence.

1. Alexander Graham Bell was an American inventor ______

2. Did you know he invented the telephone in 1876 ______

3. What a useful invention that was ______

4. Try to name another American inventor ______

5. Have you ever heard of Garrett A. Morgan ______

6. He was the inventor of the traffic light ______

7. Imagine the traffic problems we'd have without it ______

8. Matthias Baldwin built a locomotive called *Old Ironsides* ______

9. Find out what else Baldwin invented ______

10. William Seward Burroughs developed the first recording adding machine ______

11. Do you enjoy photography ______

12. Be thankful that George Eastman invented the film for your camera ______

13. How easy it is to take pictures today ______

14. Think of an invention that could make life easier ______

15. Would you like to be an inventor someday ______

Name ______________________ Date ____________

Lesson 6

Kinds of Sentences

More Practice

Using Different Kinds of Sentences

Add the correct end punctuation to each of these sentences. Then rewrite the sentences according to the instructions in parentheses. You may have to add or delete words and change word order.

CHAPTER 1

EXAMPLE Did Thomas Edison make the first light bulb?
(Change to a declarative sentence.)
Thomas Edison made the first light bulb.

1. How useful the invention of the light bulb was
(Change to a declarative sentence.)

____

2. Thomas Edison was born in 1847
(Change to an interrogative sentence.)

____

3. Will you tell me what Edison's first job was
(Change to an imperative sentence.)

____

4. Edison was a creative thinker
(Change to an exclamatory sentence.)

____

5. What a tremendous effect Edison's inventions have had on the world
(Change to a declarative sentence.)

____

6. Was Edison the inventor of the phonograph too
(Change to a declarative sentence.)

____

7. Edison's laboratory was in New Jersey
(Change to an interrogative sentence.)

____

Name ______________________________ Date ______________

Lesson 6

Kinds of Sentences

Application

CHAPTER 1

A. Writing Different Kinds of Sentences

Suppose you could meet one of the great inventors, such as Thomas Edison. Write what you might say in that situation. Use at least one of each kind of sentence: declarative, interrogative, imperative, and exclamatory. Use correct punctuation at the end of each sentence.

B. Writing Different Kinds of Sentences in a Diary

Choose a character in a book you have read or a movie you have seen. Pretend to be that character, and write a diary entry for one day in that character's life. Use at least one of each kind of sentence: declarative, interrogative, imperative, and exclamatory. Use the correct punctuation at the end of each sentence.

Name ____________________ Date ____________

Lesson 7

Subjects in Unusual Order

Teaching

CHAPTER 1

In most **questions,** the subject comes after the verb or between parts of the verb phrase.

Are you healthy? (*you* is the subject; *are* is the verb)

Do you have agility? (*you* is the subject; *Do have* is the verb phrase)

The subject of a **command,** or imperative sentence, is usually *you.* Often, *you* doesn't appear in the sentence because it is implied, or understood.

Practice that maneuver.

VERB (The implied subject is *you.*)

In an inverted sentence, the subject comes after the verb.

Up the mountain climbed the brave hiker.

VERB SUBJECT

In some sentences beginning with the words *here* or *there,* the subject follows the verb. You find the subject by looking at the words that follow the verb.

Here is a steep cliff. There were many climbers on the mountain.

VERB SUBJECT VERB SUBJECT

Finding Subjects and Verbs in Unusual Positions

In the following sentences, underline the simple subject once and the verb or verb phrase twice. If the subject is understood, write **You** in parentheses on the line.

1. Do you know anything about mountain climbing? ____________
2. There are people in love with the sport. ____________
3. Are you one of them? ____________
4. Has anyone tried that steep trail? ____________
5. Here are some suggestions for safe climbing. ____________
6. Hike with others, not alone. ____________
7. Choose your path carefully. ____________
8. There should be an emergency plan in case of danger. ____________
9. Over the sharp rocks stumbled the weary climber. ____________
10. Here comes a rockslide! ____________
11. Around the mountain climbers howled the fierce snowstorm. ____________
12. Are your hiking boots waterproof? ____________

Name ______________________________ Date ______________

Lesson 7

Subjects in Unusual Order

More Practice

A. Writing Sentences

In the following sentences, underline the simple subject once and the verb twice. Then rewrite each sentence so that the subject comes before the verb.

CHAPTER 1

EXAMPLE To the peak struggled the victorious climber.
The victorious climber struggled to the peak.

1. There are mountains under water.

____

2. In the Black Hills are dome mountains.

____

3. Were some mountains volcanic?

____

4. Far above sea level rises the mighty Mt. Everest.

____

5. Did the Rockies form after the Appalachians?

____

B. Writing Sentences

Rewrite each sentence as an inverted or imperative sentence. You may choose to add *Here* or *There.* Then underline each subject once and each verb twice in your new sentence.

EXAMPLE The miners drilled into the mountain.
Into the mountain drilled the miners.

1. The silver mine is down this shaft.

____

2. Nuggets of gold sparkled there in the mountain stream.

____

3. Coal carts rumbled through the mine entrance.

____

4. You must wear a hard hat in the mine.

____

5. Precious minerals are deep within some mountains.

____

Name ______________________________ Date ______________

Lesson 7

Subjects in Unusual Order

Application

A. Revising Using Different Sentence Orders

The writer of this paragraph decided never to use the usual word order of subject before verb. In all of the paragraph's sentences, the subject is in an unusual place or is understood. Rewrite the paragraph. Use a variety of sentence orders to improve it.

There are many attractions in the mountains. Very exciting is rock hunting. Just on the surface are different kinds of rocks. Could some of them be fossils? In the mountains live many animals also. There are small mammals and birds to study. Occasionally are seen larger animals, such as deer or moose. In a photo album can be placed pictures of these creatures. Are mountain plants important, too? On mountain meadows thrive unusual wildflowers. Think of other ways you can enjoy the mountains.

____

____

____

____

____

____

B. Revising Using a Variety of Sentence Orders

The writer of this paragraph decided always to use the usual word order of subject before verb. Rewrite the paragraph, this time using many kinds of sentence orders. Write at least two sentences in which the subject comes before the verb. Write at least two sentences in a more unusual order, with the subject after the verb.

Mountains are named by how they are formed. Sometimes the earth's crust folds like a wave. A *folded mountain* is made in this way. Often, the crust breaks into huge pieces. A *block mountain* comes from these broken pieces. Sometimes the crust rises up, but it does not fold or crack. A *dome mountain* results from the bulging crust. Occasionally, lava and ash pour out of a crack in the earth. A *volcanic mountain* is formed in this way.

____

____

____

____

____

____

CHAPTER 1

Name ______________________ Date ______________

Lesson 8 Complements: Subject Complements *Teaching*

A complement is a word or group of words that completes the meaning of the verb.

A **subject complement** is a word or group of words that follows a linking verb and renames or describes the subject. Common **linking verbs** include forms of *be,* such as *am, is, are, was, were, being,* and *been;* and verbs such as *appear, feel, look, sound, smell, seem,* and *taste.*

CHAPTER 1

Both nouns and adjectives can serve as subject complements.

A predicate noun follows a linking verb and defines or renames the subject.

The dessert is chocolate cake. (The predicate noun does not include modifiers.)
SUBJECT LINKING VERB PREDICATE NOUN

A predicate adjective follows a linking verb and describes a quality of the subject.

The dessert tastes delicious after the meal. (The predicate adjective usually does not include prepositional phrases.)
SUBJECT LINKING VERB PREDICATE ADJECTIVE

Identifying Linking Verbs and Subject Complements

In the following sentences, underline the linking verbs once and the subject complements twice. On the line, write **PA** for predicate adjective or **PN** for predicate noun.

1. Food is a basic need. ______

2. The variety of foods seems incredible! ______

3. Rice is a main dish in Asia. ______

4. Fish is the "meat" of the Pacific Islands. ______

5. In Argentina, beef is quite common. ______

6. Of all prepared foods, pancakes may be the oldest. ______

7. Tortillas are corn "pancakes." ______

8. Tortillas with meat, cheese, and hot salsa taste spicy. ______

9. The Italian word for pie is *pizza.* ______

10. Pizza remains popular throughout the world. ______

11. Many fruits are favorite snacks. ______

12. Fruits, such as peaches and apples, taste sweet. ______

13. Dairy products are important in many cultures. ______

14. Milk is a source of calcium. ______

15. A good diet is important. ______

Name ______________________________ Date ______________

Lesson 8

Complements: Subject Complements

More Practice

CHAPTER 1

A. Identifying Types of Subject Complements

In each of the following sentences, underline the linking verb once and the subject complement twice. Then, in the blank, write **PN** if the subject complement is a predicate noun or **PA** if it is a predicate adjective.

EXAMPLE The dessert is delicious. *PA*

1. My grandfather is a great baker. ________

2. His chocolate chip cookies are a real treat. ________

3. His brownies are famous in her neighborhood. ________

4. His specialty is homemade raisin bread. ________

5. That bread is incredibly tasty. ________

6. His blueberry muffins always look scrumptious! ________

7. His apple pies are masterpieces. ________

8. My grandfather's devil's food cake tastes heavenly! ________

9. His biscuits are amazingly light. ________

10. Unfortunately, many of his recipes remain secret. ________

B. Using Subject Complements

Complete each sentence below. First complete it with a predicate noun. Then complete it with a predicate adjective.

EXAMPLE The meal was *pepperoni pizza*.
The meal was *extremely spicy*.

1. The cook is ____________________

The cook is ____________________.

2. The main course was ____________________.

The main course was ____________________.

3. The table was ____________________.

The table was ____________________.

4. The guests were ____________________.

The guests were ____________________.

Name ______________________________ Date ______________

Lesson 8

Complements: Subject Complements

Application

A. Writing Subject Complements

Rewrite each of the numbered sentences in the passage below with a new subject complement. Underline your new subject complement. If it is a predicate noun, write **PN** in parentheses after the sentence. If it is a predicate adjective, write **PA.**

(1) Trying new foods is an adventure. **(2)** My favorite food is Italian. **(3)** Mexican foods taste too spicy for me. **(4)** Frogs' legs are an exotic food. **(5)** Such a dish would be interesting to eat. **(6)** A chef must be patient with his or her customers!

1. ______________________________

2. ______________________________

3. ______________________________

4. ______________________________

5. ______________________________

6. ______________________________

B. Writing with Subject Complements

Imagine that you are a food critic who reviews restaurant food in different places. Write six sentences about a restaurant you recently visited. Three of the sentences should have predicate adjectives. Three should have predicate nouns.

1. ______________________________

____

2. ______________________________

____

3. ______________________________

____

4. ______________________________

____

5. ______________________________

____

6. ______________________________

____

Name ______________________ Date ____________

Lesson 9

Complements: Objects of Verbs

Teaching

Action verbs often need complements called direct objects and indirect objects to complete their meaning.

A **direct object** is a word or a group of words that names the receiver of the verb's action. It answers the question *what?* or *whom?*

Gayle sent seashells from Florida. (*What* did Gayle send? Seashells)

An **indirect object** is a word or group of words that tells *to what, or whom,* or *for whom* an action is done. The indirect object usually comes between the verb and the direct object. Verbs that are often followed by an indirect object include *ask, bring, give, hand, lend, make, offer, send, show, teach, tell,* and *write.*

Gayle brought Tina seashells from Florida. (*For whom* did Gayle bring the seashells? Tina)

CHAPTER 1

Recognizing Objects of Verbs

In each sentence, if the underlined word is a direct object, write **DO** on the line. If it is an indirect object, write **IO.**

EXAMPLE The diver found a shipwreck. DO

1. The U.S. basketball team won the gold medal. ______
2. The Maxwells offered Cher a glass of lemonade. ______
3. France sold Louisiana to the United States. ______
4. Please send me the latest issue of your magazine. ______
5. Our school sponsored a carnival last spring.
6. We hung a wreath on our door. ______
7. The principal awarded the co-captains the trophy. ______
8. Lydia gave Michelle some good advice. ______
9. Pat got a digital watch for his birthday. ______
10. Marta made us a Mexican dinner. ______
11. The messenger handed Mr. Bronson a sealed envelope. ______
12. I carefully answered every question on the test. ______
13. The opera fans gave the singer long-stemmed roses. ______
14. Arnita telephoned Mia last night. ______
15. Lauren mailed her friends postcards from Canada. ______

Name ______________________________ Date ______________

Lesson 9

Complements: Objects of Verbs

More Practice

CHAPTER 1

A. Identifying Objects of Verbs

Identify the function of the boldfaced word in each sentence below. Write **DO** for direct object and **IO** for indirect object. If the word is not the direct object or the indirect object, write **N.**

1. A hurricane is a powerful, swirling **storm.** __________
2. Meteorologists watched a big **storm** carefully. __________
3. Newscasters gave their **listeners** warnings about the hurricane. __________
4. The hurricane struck **land** in the morning. __________
5. The hurricane winds swirled around the eye of the **storm.** __________
6. The hurricane caused huge **waves.** __________
7. The waves produced widespread **floods.** __________
8. The floodwaters destroyed many people's **property.** __________
9. Television newscasts showed their **audiences** pictures of the storm. __________
10. Volunteers sent the hurricane **victims** emergency supplies. __________

B. Using Indirect Objects

Underline the direct object in each sentence below. Then rewrite each sentence, adding an indirect object. Use a different indirect object for every sentence.

1. The mayor gave a medal for bravery.

   ____

2. Adam cooked supper.

   ____

3. Amber bought a birthday gift.

   ____

4. The salesperson showed a new style of camera.

   ____

5. The juggler showed some tricks.

   ____

Name ______________________ Date ____________

Lesson 9

Complements: Objects of Verbs

Application

A. Using Objects of Verbs

Choose one word from each list below to complete each sentence. Use each word only once. Each sentence should have both an indirect object and a direct object. If you wish, you can add words to make the sentences more interesting.

Use as indirect object	**Use as direct object**
the cooks	their trophies
the receiver	a question
her sick grandmother	their test papers
their guests	his beef stew recipe
the winners	a discount
its customers	cheese and crackers
the candidate	a pass
the students	a get-well card

1. The quarterback threw ______________________.

2. The reporter asked ______________________.

3. The gymnastics judge awarded ______________________.

4. Mrs. Ryan handed ______________________.

5. The famous chef gave ______________________.

6. The store offered ______________________.

7. Jean sent ______________________.

8. The Reynolds served ______________________.

B. Writing Sentences with Objects of Verbs

Complete each sentence with a direct and an indirect object. Use a different direct and indirect object in every sentence.

Example The chef made *her customers a lemon pie*.

1. Our grandmother sent ______________________.

2. The gardener gave ______________________.

3. The delivery person brought ______________________.

4. The basketball player handed ______________________.

5. The judge told ______________________.

Name ______________________________ Date ______________

Lesson 10

Fragments and Run-Ons

Teaching

CHAPTER 1

Sentence fragments and run-on sentences are writing errors that can make your writing difficult to understand.

A **sentence fragment** is part of a sentence that is written as if it were a complete sentence. A sentence fragment is missing a subject, a predicate, or both.

Fragments Colonists in Indian costume. (missing a predicate)
Dumped chests of tea into Boston Harbor. (missing a subject)
On December 16, 1773. (missing both)

Revision Colonists in Indian costume dumped chests of tea into Boston Harbor on December 16, 1773.

A run-on sentence is two or more sentences written as if they were a single sentence. When you combine two sentences with a conjunction, use a comma before the conjunction.

Run-on The British tried to make the colonists pay taxes they resisted.

Revision The British tried to make the colonists pay taxes, but they resisted.

Identifying Sentences, Sentence Fragments, and Run-Ons

On the short line at the right of each word group below, write **CS, F,** or **RO** to identify the word group as a complete sentence, a fragment, or a run-on sentence.

1. British soldiers marched toward Concord, Massachusetts. ______
2. They hoped to capture arms stored in Concord, Paul Revere and William Dawes raced to warn the colonists. ______
3. The Minutemen from nearby towns. ______
4. Waited for the British in Lexington. ______
5. Clashes in Lexington and Concord started the American Revolution. ______
6. George Washington became the army's commander-in-chief he took command on July 3, 1775. ______
7. Poorly trained and without uniforms. ______
8. The Declaration of Independence was adopted on July 4, 1776 it was written by Thomas Jefferson. ______
9. A young officer, Nathan Hale. ______
10. Hale was hanged by the British as a spy he became a hero to the Americans. ______
11. France joined the war as an ally of the Americans. ______
12. The British were defeated at the battle of Yorktown it meant the end of the war. ______

Name ______________________________ Date ______________

Lesson 10

Fragments and Run-Ons

More Practice

CHAPTER 1

A. Identifying and Correcting Fragments and Run-Ons

On the line after each word group below, write **CS, F,** or **RO** to identify the word group as a complete sentence, a fragment, or a run-on sentence. Then rewrite each fragment or run-on as one or more correct sentences. Add sentence parts as needed.

1. Because of the bad weather.

____

2. The boys rode the roller coaster five times in a row.

____

3. The curtain opened the show began.

____

4. Explained the rules of the game.

____

5. This restaurant serves great pizza let's eat here.

____

B. Correcting Fragments and Run-ons

Rewrite this paragraph, correcting each fragment and run-on. You may add words to any fragment to make it a sentence, or you may combine it with another sentence. To correct a run-on, you may either separate the sentences or join them correctly.

Patrick Henry failed as a storekeeper and a farmer he became a lawyer. He became famous. As an orator. Patrick Henry delivered a speech protesting the Stamp Tax it was one of his greatest speeches. During a speech in 1775. Henry pretended to stab himself with a letter opener he cried, "Give me liberty or give me death!" Henry became governor. Of Virginia. In 1776. He was re-elected governor four times.

____

____

____

____

____

____

____

Name ______________________________ Date ______________

Lesson 10

Fragments and Run-Ons

Application

CHAPTER 1

A. Proofreading for Fragments and Run-Ons

Rewrite this paragraph, correcting each fragment and run-on. You may add words to any fragment to make it a sentence, or you may combine it with another sentence. To correct a run-on, you may either separate the sentences or join them correctly.

During the American Revolution, Great Britain had an army of well-trained soldiers the British soldier had a hard life. He rarely had much food. Was often moldy. His uniform was attractive. Was not practical. His hat did not offer much protection from the sun his suits were heavy. And hot. On one summer march. Near New York City. Sixty-three soldiers collapsed from heatstroke.

____

____

____

____

____

____

____

B. Recognizing and Revising Fragments and Run-ons

Read these notes one student wrote to use in a report. First figure out what the writer was going to say, and then use the information to write a paragraph. Use complete sentences instead of fragments and run-on sentences. Add any words that you need to make the paragraph understandable.

Children around the world enjoy playing with dolls adults enjoy dolls too. Many grown-ups collect antique dolls others collect costume dolls. As a hobby. The first dolls for children were made in the 1700s they looked and were dressed like adults. The first dolls that looked like babies. Appeared about 1850. Antique dolls are rare and expensive. Sell for thousands of dollars. Many museums huge doll collections.

____

____

____

____

____

____

____

Name ______________________________ Date ______________

Lesson 1

Kinds of Nouns

Teaching

A **noun** is a word that names a person, place, thing, or idea. Examples are *leader, Virginia, colony,* and *exploration.*

A **common noun** is a general name for a person, place, thing, or idea. A **proper noun** is the name of a particular person, place, thing, or idea. For example, *settler* is a common noun; *John Alden* is a proper noun. Only proper nouns need to be capitalized.

A **concrete noun** names a thing that can be seen, heard, smelled, tasted, or touched. An **abstract noun** names an idea, feeling, quality, or characteristic. Examples of concrete nouns are *cabin* and *log;* examples of abstract nouns are *danger* and *bravery.*

A **collective noun** is a word that names a group of people or things, such as *crew.*

CHAPTER 2

A. Identifying Nouns

Underline all the nouns in the following sentences. Every sentence has more than one.

1. Ms. Enriquez believes wealth cannot bring happiness.
2. Baseball is sometimes called the game of summer.
3. The jury awarded money to the victims of the crime.
4. Does Tim live in a house or an apartment?
5. In the movie, a band of outlaws rustled the herd of cattle.

B. Identifying Proper and Common Nouns

Underline all the nouns in the following sentences. Write P above the proper nouns. Write **C** above the common nouns.

EXAMPLE The disappearance (C) of settlers (C) on Roanoke Island (P) remains a mystery (C).

1. A group of explorers from Spain settled in St. Augustine, Florida.
2. Sir Francis Drake of England sailed around the world in a small ship called the *Golden Hind.*
3. Queen Isabella had high hopes for the success of Christopher Columbus.
4. The Aztecs, Incas, and Mayas lived within large empires.
5. One important accomplishment was the exploration of the Mississippi River.

C. Identifying Types of Nouns

Review the underlined nouns in the sentences in the above exercises. Find and list the nouns requested on the lines below.

1. Two collective nouns in Exercise A, sentence 5 ______________________
2. Two common, concrete nouns in Exercise B, sentence 2 ______________________
3. Two common, abstract nouns in Exercise B, sentence 3 ______________________

Name ______________________ Date ____________

Lesson 1 Kinds of Nouns

More Practice

A. Identifying Nouns

Underline all the nouns in each of the following sentences. On each line below, write one of the nouns that match the description in parentheses.

1. The colony at Plymouth faced many dangers during the first winter.

   (proper) ____________ (common) ____________

2. The story of Pocahontas and her brave act may not be entirely factual.

   (concrete) ____________ (abstract) ____________

3. The congregation of Puritans longed for religious freedom.

   (collective) ____________ (proper) ____________

4. Some tribes shared common beliefs with the settlers.

   (collective) ____________ (abstract) ____________

5. William Bradford worked with Massasoit to insure peace.

   (proper) ____________ (abstract) ____________

CHAPTER 2

B. Using Nouns

Rewrite the following sentences, replacing each boldfaced common noun with a proper noun. Each new noun should reflect the same idea or subject as the boldfaced noun. You may need to change some words, such as *a, an,* and *the.*

EXAMPLE Did you see a boy in a red T-shirt skate down **the street?**
Did you see a boy in a red T-shirt skate down Hill Street?

1. My friend is looking forward to seeing a **film** at the Garden Theater.

   ____

2. Our social studies teacher showed us maps of the **country.**

   ____

3. Kate took an express train to a large **city.**

   ____

4. That store is a good place to buy the **newspaper.**

   ____

5. A celebration of the **holiday** was held at Central Park.

   ____

Name ______________________ Date ____________

Lesson 1

Kinds of Nouns

Application

A. Finding Nouns

Underline the noun or nouns described in parentheses after each sentence. Also, identify every proper noun by writing the capital letter over the first letter of the word.

1. The first settlement in america was not at plymouth rock. (common)

2. A desire for wealth lured the first spaniards to america. (abstract)

3. One band of adventurers founded the town of st. augustine, florida. (collective)

4. The union of the lands claimed by spain and england came much later. (abstract)

5. Visitors to that town in florida can see houses built in the old style. (concrete)

6. On a chilly day in december, a group of pilgrims landed at plymouth. (collective)

7. Their courage is admired by americans even today. (abstract)

8. Do you know who taught the settlers how to plant corn? (concrete)

9. The pilgrims hoped for friendship with the natives but were not always fair to them. (abstract)

10. Pocahontas was captured by the english and given a new name. (common)

CHAPTER 2

B. Using Nouns

First write at least two nouns of each type identified. Then write a sentence using the nouns. Underline all the nouns in your sentence.

Example common and abstract *liberty, bravery*
Americans enjoy liberty because of the bravery of early colonists.

1. proper and concrete ______________________

____

2. collective ______________________

____

3. common and concrete ______________________

____

4. common and abstract ______________________

____

5. proper ______________________

____

Name ______________________________ Date ____________

Lesson 2 Singular and Plural Nouns

Teaching

A **singular noun** names one person, place, thing, or idea. A **plural noun** names more than one person, place, thing, or idea.

One inventor had an outlandish suggestion. (singular nouns)
Several inventors had outlandish suggestions. (plural nouns)

This chart shows the usual ways to form the plurals of nouns.

Singular	Rule	Sample Plural
desk, chair	Add *-s* to most nouns.	desks, chairs
brush, box	Add *-es* to nouns ending in *s, sh, ch, x,* or *z.*	brushes, boxes
radio, stereo echo, hero	Add *-s* to most nouns that end in *o.* Add *-es* to a few nouns that end in *o.*	radios, stereos echoes, heroes
hobby, fly monkey, day	Change the *y* to an *i* and add *-es* to most nouns ending in *y.* If a vowel comes before the y, add -s.	hobbies, flies monkeys, days
shelf, knife roof, cuff	Change the *f* to a *v* and add *-es* to most nouns that end in *f* or *fe.* Add *-s* to a few nouns that end in *f* or *fe.*	shelves, knives roofs, cuffs
sheep, tuna	Some nouns keep the same spelling.	sheep, tuna
woman, foot	The plural forms of some nouns are irregular.	women, feet

CHAPTER 2

A. Identifying Plural Forms of Nouns

In each sentence, underline only the plural nouns.

1. Do you see the dark puffs of smoke coming from those chimneys?
2. Signs warn motorists of deer on the road.
3. Farmers had a good crop of cherries this year.
4. Small inns and farmhouses dotted the roads.
5. Miguel pointed out monuments honoring heroes of the war.

B. Correcting Errors in Plural Nouns

In each sentence, the boldfaced plural has been formed incorrectly. Write the correctly spelled plural on the line.

1. How beautiful to see the **leafs** changing colors! ____________
2. We stopped at a picnic area to eat our **sandwichs.** ____________
3. Mom cut up fresh **tomatos** from a farmer's fruit stand. ____________
4. Some country bridges are only ten **foots** high. ____________
5. Truck **driveres** could have problems on those bridges. ____________

Name ______________________ Date ____________

Lesson 2

Singular and Plural Nouns

More Practice

A. Identifying Plural Forms of Nouns

In each sentence, underline only the plural nouns.

1. Many sheep and horses grazed in the fields.

2. There were cows and calves near the fence.

3. We looked out the windows at the healthy crops.

4. Look at that flock of geese across the road!

5. Some farmers sell potatoes and other vegetables.

6. You don't hear stereos and the sounds of beeping horns in the country.

CHAPTER 2

B. Correcting Errors in Plural Nouns

In each sentence, find and underline the plural that has been formed incorrectly. Write the correctly spelled plural on the line.

1. We will have many storys to tell after our camping trips. ____________

2. Several deers approached our campsites. ____________

3. Do the buzzs of those bees frighten you? ____________

4. Fred and Lisa took many photoes with their new cameras. ____________

5. Dad was hoping to catch several bass and trouts for our suppers. ____________

6. I hope our stereoes don't frighten the animals. ____________

7. Let's keep our food items several foots above the ground. ____________

8. Where are the three boxs of potato chips? ____________

9. The berries on those bushs look good for eating. ____________

10. Our motheres will be pleased if we bring back enough for some pies. ____________

C. Using Plural Nouns

Form the plural of the given nouns. Then use all three plurals in a single sentence.

1. wife ____________ city ____________ potato ____________

____

2. boy ____________ sandwich ____________ loaf ____________

____

3. goose ____________ field ____________ grass ____________

____

Name ______________________ Date ____________

Lesson 2

Singular and Plural Nouns

Application

A. Identifying Uses of Plural Nouns

In the following sentences, decide whether each noun is in the correct form, singular or plural. If the noun should be plural, has the plural been formed correctly? Rewrite every sentence with the correct noun forms.

1. The three fishermens caught at least eight tunas.

____

2. We tasted several dish from countrys around the world at the cookout.

____

3. Tanya changed the recipe by substituting tomatos and bay leafs.

____

4. Fay and Ken used little knifes to cut ten peach.

____

CHAPTER 2

B. Using Plural Nouns

Form the plural of the given nouns. Then use all three plurals in a single sentence.

1. man ________ animal ________ leash ________

2. radio ________ shelf ________ hobby ________

3. team ________ box ________ coach________

____

C. Using Nouns

Suppose that your class is making a time capsule for people to open in 50 years. What items would you like people in the future to see so they would have an idea of how you live your life today? Write a short paragraph describing what you would put in the box. Underline at least six plural nouns in your paragraph.

____

____

____

____

____

____

____

Name ______________________________ Date ______________

Lesson 3

Possessive Nouns

Teaching

The **possessive form** of a noun shows ownership or relationship. For example, *wren's nest* (ownership); *Mom's friend* (relationship).

You may use possessive nouns in place of longer phrases.

> Did you attend the concert <u>of the scout troop</u>?
> Did you attend the <u>scout troop's</u> concert?

The following chart shows the usual ways to form possessive nouns.

	Noun	Rule	Possessive
Singular:	bird	Add an apostrophe and *-s*	bird's family
Plural ending in *-s:*	eggs	Add an apostrophe	eggs' colors
Plurals not ending in *-s:*	men	Add an apostrophe and *-s*	men's hats

CHAPTER 2

A. Identifying Possessive Nouns

Underline each possessive noun. On the blank, write **S** if that noun is singular or **P** if it is plural.

1. The children's chorus held a performance in the gymnasium. ______

2. Several classes' gym periods had to be canceled. ______

3. We listened to our music teacher's introduction. ______

4. James's mother offered to find volunteers to work the after-concert reception. ______

5. Two men's coats were misplaced at the reception. ______

6. One soloist's voice stood out above all the rest. ______

B. Using Possessive Nouns

Complete each sentence with the possessive form of the word shown in parentheses.

1. Two ____________________ guitar strings broke during the rehearsal. (musicians)

2. I would like to learn to play several ____________________ work. (pianists)

3. Everybody seems to enjoy ____________________ music. (Mozart)

4. One ____________________ voice was particularly beautiful. (soprano)

5. Several famous orchestra ____________________ batons were on display. (leaders)

6. Reporters printed many ____________________ reactions to the concert. (people)

Name ______________________________ Date ______________

Lesson 3

Possessive Nouns

More Practice

A. Identifying Possessive Nouns

Underline the possessive noun in each sentence. If a possessive has been formed incorrectly, write the correctly spelled word on the line. If a possessive has been spelled correctly, write **C.**

1. A clarinets' keys make it look complicated. ______________

2. I bought a harmonica with last weekses' allowance. ______________

3. Mom's opinion is that loud music will harm my hearing. ______________

4. A musicians' day is filled with hours of practice. ______________

5. Many songwriteres' incomes come from royalties. ______________

6. That songs' popularity has made it a holiday classic for decades. ______________

7. I can't get that tunes' melody out of my mind. ______________

8. Mr. Ross's nephew will play the song at the winter concert. ______________

9. Peoples's opinions about music can vary. ______________

10. Stores such as Sam's Music Mart carry many kinds of recordings for all tastes. ______________

CHAPTER 2

B. Using Possessive Nouns in Sentences

On the line to the right, rewrite the given phrase as a possessive noun. Then use the possessive in a sentence.

Example the music of Johann Bach *Johann Bach's music*
*My father likes **Johann Bach's** music.*

1. music skills of my teacher ______________

____

2. audience of the choral group ______________

____

3. voices of some jazz singers ______________

____

4. giggling of children ______________

____

Name ________________________________ Date ______________

Lesson 3

Possessive Nouns

Application

A. Using Possessive Nouns in Sentences

Underline each phrase that can be rewritten using a possessive noun. Then rewrite the sentences using those possessive nouns.

1. The preference of my piano teacher is classical music.

____

2. The nickname of Louis Armstrong was "Satchmo."

____

3. How did audiences respond to the songs of Satchmo?

____

4. The cheers of the audience tell you how well received his music was.

____

5. The voice of a soprano is higher than the voice of an alto.

____

6. The success of a musician does not happen overnight.

____

B. Using Possessive Nouns in Writing

You are the chairperson of a toy drive for needy children. Imagine that you have a committee of five students working with you. Tell how the toys will be collected and who will receive them. Underline at least five possessive nouns in your paragraph.

____

____

____

____

____

____

____

____

____

____

____

Lesson 4

Compound Nouns

Teaching

A **compound noun** is made up of two or more words used together as a single noun.

Compound nouns can be written in one of three ways:

One single word: *windshield*
Two or more separate words: *air bag*
A hyphenated word: *two-seater*

The following chart shows the usual ways to form the plurals of compound nouns.

	Singular	Rule	Plural
One word	townhouse	Add *-s* to most words	townhouses
	hairbrush	Add *-es* to words that end in *ch, sh, s, x,* or *z.*	hairbrushes
Two or more words or hyphenated words	traffic light mother-in-law	Make the main noun plural.	traffic lights mothers-in-law

A. Identifying Compound Nouns

Underline every compound noun in the following sentences.

1. Did you see the moving van parked in our neighbor's driveway?

2. The school board voted for safety belts on buses.

3. My sister-in-law recently bought a car so she could drive it to her new job at the department store.

4. You can catch the cable car at a stop on Market Street.

5. The steering wheel on that car is covered with cowhide.

B. Using Plural Compound Nouns

Underline the compound nouns that are spelled incorrectly. Rewrite the sentences, using the correct plural form of those nouns.

1. Two carwashs are located on Main Street.

____

2. Dad's brother-in-laws both have red sports cars.

____

3. Some mother-to-bes are interested in buying antique high chairs for their babies.

____

4. In our state, 16-years-old cannot drive alone.

____

Name ______________________________ Date ______________

Lesson 4

Compound Nouns

More Practice

A. Identifying Compound Nouns

Underline every singular compound noun once. Underline every plural compound noun twice.

1. The moonlight glistened off the lake.
2. Do your grandparents own a bed-and-breakfast?
3. The snowstorm left the travelers stranded with only farmhouses in sight.
4. They waited until after dinnertime to ask the homeowners if they could use their telephone.
5. The attendant at the gas station said he would send a towtruck.
6. The travelers slept in small bunkbeds at a motel until their car was repaired.
7. Days later, they were glad to see the skyline of their city and all the skyscrapers that meant home to them.

CHAPTER 2

B. Using Compound Nouns

Write the plural forms for each set of compound words. Then use all three plural compounds in a single sentence.

1. airplane ______________

   airport ______________

   luggage cart ______________

   ____

   ____

2. thunderstorm ______________

   raincloud ______________

   brother-in-law ______________

   ____

   ____

3. president-elect ______________

   swimsuit ______________

   swimming pool ______________

   ____

   ____

Name ______________________ Date ______________

Lesson 4

Compound Nouns

Application

A. Using Compound Nouns

Rewrite the following sentences, replacing each boldfaced phrase with a compound noun. You will need to drop some words to be sure your new sentences sound right.

EXAMPLE Our neighbor owns a *van used for moving.*
Our neighbor owns a moving van.

1. Carl's brother-in-law has a **throat that is sore.**

____

2. Please pull down the **shade for a window** near the front door.

____

3. A **storm with thunder** is predicted for this afternoon.

____

4. Which **grounds to camp on** are your family's favorites?

____

5. Those **shelves for books** may not hold these heavy volumes.

____

6. The **park filled with amusements** has a new, faster roller coaster.

____

CHAPTER 2

B. Using Compound Nouns in Writing

Write a news article reporting on a contest in which there was one winner and two runners-up. Describe the activities in the contest, where the contest took place, and the prizes that were awarded. Use at least five compound nouns in your article. Underline each compound noun that you use.

____

____

____

____

____

____

____

____

____

Name ______________________________ Date ______________

Lesson 5

Nouns as Subjects and Complements

Teaching

In sentences, **nouns** have different jobs.

As the subject, a noun tells whom or what the sentence is about.

<u>Marie</u> reads the map on car trips. <u>Vacations</u> are fun for her family.

As the **complement,** a noun completes the meaning of the sentence. This chart shows how a noun may work as a **predicate noun,** a **direct object,** or an **indirect object.**

Nouns as Complements		
Predicate noun	renames or defines the subject after a linking verb	Mr. Morell is a **pilot.**
Direct object	names the receiver of the action of the action verb	Our family bought an **atlas.**
Indirect object	tells *to whom or what* or *for whom or what* an action is done	The airline sent the **tourists** their tickets.

CHAPTER 2

Identifying Nouns Used as Subjects and Complements

In each sentence, identify the word in bold type. On the blank, write **S** for subject, **PN** for predicate noun, **DO** for direct object, and **IO** for indirect object.

1. **Denmark** is a country in northern Europe. ______
2. Our teacher visited **Copenhagen** on his vacation. ______
3. Mr. Swanson showed the **class** slides of his trip. ______
4. The Tivoli is a huge **park** with restaurants and entertainment. ______
5. The **Swansons** saw a statue of the Little Mermaid. ______
6. She was a **character** in a story by Hans Christian Andersen. ______
7. Alex checked out some travel **books** from the library. ______
8. Mr. Langley is the **librarian** in charge of research. ______
9. He gave **Alex** some valuable advice about travel. ______
10. Laura chose some **videos** about Norway. ______
11. **Dad** was a sailor over 20 years ago, stationed in Europe. ______
12. Norway was one **country** that he visited at that time. ______
13. The whole family is planning next summer's **trip.** ______
14. Frank sent his **cousin** in Norway a letter. ______

Name ____________________ Date ____________

Lesson 5

Nouns as Subjects and Complements

More Practice

A. Identifying Nouns as Complements

Underline the subject of each sentence. Then identify the complement in bold type. Write **PN** for predicate noun, **DO** for direct object, or **IO** for indirect object.

1. The capital of France is **Paris.** ______
2. The Wrights took an overseas **flight** that left Thursday evening. ______
3. Ted gave **Dad** his carry-on while we waited for the luggage. ______
4. A uniformed man was holding a **sign** with their name on it at the airport. ______
5. Our tour guide for the week was **Simone.** ______
6. The tourists loved the **sight** of the Eiffel Tower at night. ______
7. The Louvre is a world-famous art **museum.** ______
8. The guide gave **members** of the group their tickets for the boat ride. ______
9. Mom sent our cousins **postcards** of the Mona Lisa. ______
10. The Seine is a major **river** in France. ______

B. Using Nouns as Subjects and Complements

Complete each sentence with a noun. Then write **S** if the noun you have supplied is used as a subject; **PN** if it is used as a predicate noun; **DO** if it is used as a direct object; and **IO** if it is used as an indirect object.

Example The *library* is located on the corner of Main and Elm. *S*

1. The principal gave ____________ a certificate for perfect attendance. ______
2. The magician did a ____________ that amazed his audience. ______
3. Basketball is a ____________ that requires endurance. ______
4. After the rain, ____________ crawled out onto the sidewalk. ______
5. The artist sold a ____________ of the house where she grew up. ______
6. The bride threw her ____________ her bouquet. ______
7. Sleeping Beauty is a very old ____________ from Europe. ______

CHAPTER 2

Name ______________________ Date __________

Lesson 5

Nouns as Subjects and Complements

Application

A. Using Nouns as Subjects and Complements

Complete each sentence with a noun. Then write **S** If the noun you have supplied is used as a subject; write **PN** if it is used as a predicate noun; **DO** if it is used as a direct object; or **IO** if it is used as an indirect object.

EXAMPLE Mrs. Petros told ___Helen___ a good story about her trip. IO

1. The city of Athens is an exciting __________ to visit. _____
2. It has many ancient __________, such as the Acropolis. _____
3. Greece is a __________ in eastern Europe, bordering the Mediterranean Sea. _____
4. One beautiful __________ was built at the top of a hill overlooking the city. _____
5. People climb many __________ to get to the top of the hill. _____
6. Some tourists take a __________ from downtown Athens to the Parthenon. _____
7. Theodore sent __________ a postcard from Rhodes, Greece. _____
8. Most __________ love the warm weather in Greece. _____

B. Using Nouns as Complements in Writing

Write a letter to a pen pal who lives in another city or country. Invite that person to come for a visit to your hometown. Describe some sights you would like to show him or her. In your letter, include at least two predicate nouns, two nouns used as direct objects, and one noun used as an indirect object. Underline those nouns in your letter and label them by writing **PN, DO,** or **IO** above each one.

CHAPTER 2

Name ______________________________ Date ______________

Lesson 6

Nouns in Phrases

Teaching

Nouns often appear in prepositional phrases and appositive phrases. These phrases add information to the sentence.

An **object of a preposition** is the noun or pronoun that follows the preposition.

> Dina enjoys cooking food <u>from other **countries**</u>.
>
> (The preposition is *from*; the object of the preposition is the noun *countries;* the prepositional phrase is *from other countries.*)

An **appositive** is a noun or pronoun that identifies or renames another noun or pronoun. An **appositive phrase** is made up of an appositive and its modifiers.

> Biscotti, <u>crisp **cookies**</u>, are loved by children in Italy.
>
> (The appositive is the noun *cookies;* the appositive phrase is *crisp cookies.*)

CHAPTER 2

Appositive phrases that provide information that isn't essential to the understanding of the preceding noun should be separated from the rest of the sentence by commas.

> Jake tried borscht, <u>a Russian beet soup</u>, at the party.

Identifying Nouns Used as Objects of Prepositions and Appositives

Identify each boldfaced noun as an object of a preposition or an appositive. Write **OP** or **APP** on the line to the right.

1. We planned an international party in the **neighborhood.** ______
2. On **Sunday** every family brought a special dish to share. ______
3. Pita, thin **bread,** was stacked on a platter. ______
4. Pierre brought Brie, a French **cheese.** ______
5. Our Japanese neighbors served tempura on a large **platter.** ______
6. Chicken, beans, and cheese are good fillings for **burritos.** ______
7. As a **topping** we used salsa and sour cream. ______
8. Our Italian neighbors provided antipasto, delicious **appetizers.** ______
9. Tandoori, a special cooking **method,** is used in India. ______
10. Our friends from **Greece** brought lamb shish kebabs. ______
11. The meat and vegetables were cooked on metal **skewers.** ______
12. Kasha, a coarsely ground **grain,** looked like porridge. ______
13. Everybody enjoyed apple strudel, a German **dessert.** ______
14. We are already planning another international food festival for next **summer.** ______

Name ______________________________ Date ______________

Lesson 6

Nouns in Phrases

More Practice

A. Identifying Nouns in Phrases

Each sentence below has either an appositive phrase or a prepositional phrase. Underline the phrase and circle its noun. On the line to the right, write **OP** if the underlined word is the object of a preposition or **APP** if it is the noun in an appositive phrase.

1. Curry, a deep yellow powder, is a popular Indian spice. ______

2. You can find curry in the spice section. ______

3. Pizza lovers have their choice of toppings. ______

4. Tortillas are often made from corn flour. ______

5. Quesadillas, cheese sandwiches, are Mexican specialties. ______

6. Appetizers are popular in every country. ______

7. Red, green, or yellow peppers can be filled with stuffing. ______

8. Baklava, a honey-soaked pastry, is a delicious dessert. ______

9. Making baklava takes a great deal of time. ______

10. Potiza, a Slovenian nutbread, is a delicious holiday treat. ______

B. Using Nouns in Phrases

Write sentences, using the prepositional phrases given in items 1, 2, and 3. Then use the phrases in items 4 and 5 as appositive phrases in original sentences.

1. around the rice

____

2. throughout dinner

____

3. between courses

____

4. a familiar ice cream flavor

____

5. a special dessert

____

CHAPTER 2

Name ______________________ Date ______________

Lesson 6

Nouns in Phrases

Application

A. Using Nouns in Phrases

Write a sentence using each noun as the object of a preposition or as the noun in an appositive phrase. Follow the directions in parentheses.

1. breakfast (Use in a prepositional phrase.)

____

2. bread (Use in a prepositional phrase.)

____

CHAPTER 2

3. dessert (Use in an appositive phrase.)

____

4. mixture (Use in an appositive phrase.)

____

5. spoon (Use in a prepositional phrase.)

____

B. Writing Nouns in Phrases

Write a paragraph explaining how to make an easy dish. It can be something as simple as a fried egg or a sandwich. If you like, you can invent a dish to make. Describe the utensils and ingredients you need to prepare the dish. Use at least two prepositional phrases and two appositive phrases in your paragraph. Underline those phrases and label them by writing **PP** or **APP** above them.

____

Name ______________________ Date ______________

Lesson 1

What Is a Pronoun?

Teaching

A **pronoun** is a word that is used in place of a noun or another pronoun. The word that a personal pronoun refers to is called its **antecedent.**

Personal pronouns change their forms to reflect **person, number,** and **case.**

Person Personal pronouns have different forms for first person, second person, and third person.

Number Pronouns can be singular or plural.

Case Personal pronouns change their forms depending on how they are used in a sentence. Each pronoun has three cases: subject, object, and possessive.

		Subject	Object	Possessive
Singular	First Person	I	me	my, mine
	Second Person	you	you	your, yours
	Third Person	he, she, it	him, her, it	his, her, hers, its
Plural	First Person	we	us	our, ours
	Second Person	you	you	your, yours
	Third Person	they	them	their, theirs

CHAPTER 3

Finding Personal Pronouns

Underline each personal pronoun in the following sentences.

1. We enjoy many stories from Greek mythology.
2. You may have heard about Persephone and how the Greeks explained the changes of the seasons.
3. She was the beautiful daughter of Demeter, the goddess of agriculture.
4. One day as she was picking flowers in the meadow, the ground opened.
5. Hades, the god of the dead, kidnapped her.
6. He took her to the underworld to be queen of his kingdom.
7. "Where is my daughter?" cried Demeter.
8. She became angry with the gods for allowing her daughter to be kidnapped.
9. She refused to allow their crops to grow.
10. The gods begged Zeus to help them.
11. Zeus asked Hades to return Persephone to her mother.
12. "But I have eaten pomegranate seeds as a sign of my marriage to Hades," said Persephone.
13. They finally came to an agreement.
14. Persephone would spend part of the year with her mother; this time would be our spring, summer, and fall.
15. She would live in the underworld the rest of the time; this time would be our winter.

Name ______________________________ Date ______________

Lesson 1

What Is a Pronoun?

More Practice

A. Finding Personal Pronouns

Underline each personal pronoun in the following sentences.

1. Greek writers and artists often called on the Muses to help them in their work.

2. They were nine goddesses of the arts and sciences.

3. Their father was Zeus, the king of the gods.

4. A poet would call on Calliope, Erato, or Euterpe to help him or her compose the perfect poem.

5. Writers of tragedy or comedy invoked Melpomene or Thalia to aid them.

6. Singers and dancers directed their pleas to Polyhymnia and Terpsichore.

7. Clio was another goddess; she was the Muse of history.

8. Urania helped scientists because her specialty was astronomy.

9. The Muses had melodic voices and often used them to sing in a chorus.

10. They lived on Mount Olympus with their leader, Apollo.

11. He, like them, remained young and beautiful forever.

12. Our words *music* and *museum* are derived from the Greek word *muse*.

CHAPTER 3

B. Using Personal Pronouns

Replace the underlined nouns in this paragraph with personal pronouns. Write the pronouns on the lines below.

Two brothers, Prometheus and Epimetheus, were members of a race of giant gods called Titans. The Titans assigned **(1)** <u>Prometheus and Epimetheus</u> the job of giving certain powers to the animals. Prometheus was angered when no gifts were left for people. **(2)** <u>Prometheus</u> stole fire from the gods and gave **(3)** <u>fire</u> to the poor people. Zeus punished Prometheus by chaining **(4)** <u>Prometheus</u> to a huge rock. Every day an eagle came and tore out **(5)** <u>Prometheus'</u> liver. At night **(6)** <u>the liver</u> would grow back.

1. ______________________

2. ______________________

3. ______________________

4. ______________________

5. ______________________

6. ______________________

Name ____________________ Date ____________

Lesson 1

What Is a Pronoun?

Application

A. Using Personal Pronouns

Rewrite this paragraph, using personal pronouns to replace some of the nouns that have been used too often. Write your revised paragraph on the lines below.

Pan was the Greek god of pastures and woods. Pan protected sheep and shepherds. Pan's body was half-man and half-goat. Ancient Greeks believed that Pan lived in lonely places, such as caves or mountains. Ancient Greeks thought Pan had a wild nature. According to ancient Greeks, Pan could fill humans with sudden terror. Pan was famous for inventing the reed panpipe. Pan played beautiful music on the panpipe.

B. Using Personal Pronouns in a Familiar Story

In your own words, retell a familiar folktale, fable, or myth that you know well, and write your version on the lines below. Be sure to use a variety of personal pronouns.

CHAPTER 3

Name ______________________________ Date ______________

Lesson 2 Subject Pronouns

Teaching

A **subject pronoun** is used as the subject of a sentence or as a predicate pronoun after a linking verb.

Singular	Plural
I	we
you	you
he, she, it	they

Subject Pronouns

Use the **subject case** of a pronoun when the pronoun is the subject of a sentence. Remember that a pronoun can be part of a compound subject.

Subject — **Susan B. Anthony believed in equal rights. She worked with others for the right to vote.** (*She* replaces *Susan B. Anthony.*)

Part of compound subject — **Susan and they won this right.**

CHAPTER 3

Use the subject case for predicate pronouns. A **predicate pronoun** follows a linking verb and renames the subject. Remember that the most common linking verbs are forms of the verb *be* and include *is, am, are, was, were, been, has been, have been, can be, will be, could be,* and *should be.*

Predicate pronoun — **A suffragist was she.**

A. Identifying Subject Pronouns

Underline all the subject pronouns in the following sentences.

1. Have you ever heard of Susan B. Anthony?
2. A leader in the woman suffrage movement was she.
3. *Suffrage* is an unusual word, but it simply means the right to vote.
4. In colonial times landowners could vote, but they were usually adult men.
5. As a landowner, he could vote in every election, but a woman could not.
6. Many women suffragists declared, "We deserve the right to vote!"

B. Using Subject Pronouns

Underline the correct pronoun to complete each sentence.

1. When Susan B. Anthony met Elizabeth Cady Stanton, (them, they) decided to work together.
2. Both Stanton and (her, she) strongly believed in equal rights.
3. (Us, We) know the two women edited a book called *History of Woman Suffrage.*
4. Close friends were (they, them).
5. Susan B. Anthony voted in the 1872 election, but (she, her) was arrested.
6. Although the judge fined her $100, (him, he) took no further action against her.
7. You and (me, I) have probably seen a one-dollar coin in honor of Ms. Anthony.

Name ______________________________ Date ______________

Lesson 2

Subject Pronouns

More Practice

A. Using Subject Pronouns

In each sentence, underline the pronoun that completes each sentence correctly.

1. In the early 1800s some men and women called for equal voting rights, but (they, them) had little success at first.
2. When Lucretia Mott and Elizabeth Cady Stanton held a convention, (it, its) attracted public attention.
3. At the convention, Lucretia and (her, she) helped write a Declaration of Sentiments.
4. A suffrage organization was formed by Lucy Stone and her husband, Henry Blackwell; (they, them) wanted states to allow women to vote.
5. Later, Lucy and (him, he) joined with other suffrage groups.
6. (Us, We) might remember Susan B. Anthony's work in the temperance movement.
7. Once at a temperance meeting run by men, (she, her) was not allowed to speak.
8. (She, Her) continued to encourage other women in temperance groups to speak out on voting rights.
9. She and (them, they) made voting rights a goal of the temperance movement.
10. When Susan B. Anthony saw that some Western states began giving women the right to vote, (she, her) was encouraged.
11. An amendment to the Constitution was introduced in Congress, but (it, its) took 40 years to pass.
12. Now, you and (I, me) can read the 19th Amendment in the Constitution granting women the right to vote.

B. Choosing Subject Pronouns

Fill in the blanks in the following sentences with appropriate subject pronouns. Vary the pronouns you use, and do not use the pronoun *you*.

1. Pat and ________________ like to play math games.
2. Did Maurice or ________________ win the spelling contest?
3. A great dancer is ________________.
4. As the sound got louder, ________________ hurt my ears.
5. ________________ did the warm-up exercises in a group.

CHAPTER 3

Name ______________________________ Date ______________

Lesson 2

Subject Pronouns

Application

A. Proofreading

Proofread the following story to make sure that subject pronouns have been used in the right places. When you find a pronoun used incorrectly, cross it out. Then insert this proofreading symbol ^ and write the correct pronoun above it.

Susan B. Anthony was born in 1820 to a Quaker family in Massachusetts. She was taught by her parents to respect everyone. Both her and them believed that men and women should have equal rights. A man could vote and could own property. A woman could do neither. When Susan got older, her and other women became active in the suffrage movement. They marched and demonstrated for a woman's right to vote. Elizabeth Cady Stanton and her wrote about woman suffrage. Often them spoke out on women's equality with men. When a few states in the West began granting women the right to vote, Susan saw a glimmer of hope. Unfortunately, she died 14 years before the 19th Amendment, granting women equal voting rights with men, was ratified. Us as Americans honored Susan B. Anthony with a special coin.

CHAPTER 3

B. Using Pronouns in Writing

Imagine that you are seeing people come into a school gym to vote. Think about all the kinds of people you might see there and write about them in a paragraph. Be sure to use subject pronouns correctly.

Name ________________________ Date ____________

Lesson 3

Object Pronouns

Teaching

Object pronouns are personal pronouns used as direct objects, as indirect objects, or as the objects of prepositions.

Object Pronouns

Singular	Plural
me	us
you	you
him, her, it	them

As a **direct object,** the pronoun receives the action of a verb and answers the question *whom* or *what.* As an **indirect object,** the pronoun tells *to whom or what* or *for whom or what* an action is performed. As an **object of a preposition,** the pronoun follows a preposition such as *to, from, for, against, by, between,* or *about.*

Direct object	The workhouse chefs made soup, and Oliver Twist thanked <u>them</u>. (Whom did he thank? them)
Indirect object	The server had the soup, and Oliver gave <u>her</u> his empty bowl. (To whom did he give his empty bowl? her)
Object of the preposition	The chef didn't give any more to <u>him</u>.

A. Identifying Object Pronouns

Underline all the object pronouns in the following sentences.

1. Oliver Twist, a character in Charles Dickens's novel, didn't have any parents; you could call him an orphan.
2. His workhouse, the place where he lived, treated him badly.
3. Because of the horrid conditions at the workhouse, he ran away from it.
4. He met a man named Fagin who promised him a place to live.
5. Fagin took care of other boys as well, but in return, he expected them to steal.
6. Oliver got caught stealing, but the end of the book will surprise you.

B. Using Object Pronouns

Underline the correct pronoun to complete each sentence.

1. David Copperfield's mother dies, and she leaves (him, he) with a cruel stepfather.
2. The stepfather knows of a shabby workhouse and sends the boy to (them, it).
3. Later Mr. Micawber gives (he, him) a home, but Mr. Micawber is soon imprisoned for debt.
4. David has an aunt and eventually goes to live with (she, her).
5. If you look at the lives of Charles Dickens and the fictional David Copperfield, you will see the similarities between (them, him).
6. Dickens's father's imprisonment for debt forced (he, him) to labor in a workhouse.

CHAPTER 3

Name ______________________________ Date ______________

Lesson 3

Object Pronouns

More Practice

A. Using Object Pronouns

In each sentence, underline the pronoun that completes each sentence correctly.

1. Ebenezer Scrooge was a crabby old man who had one clerk working for (him, he).
2. Scrooge owned a money-changing house, and therefore many people owed (he, him) money.
3. No matter what the circumstances, Scrooge was never nice or generous to (them, it) about paying the money back.
4. One night the ghost of his dead partner comes to see (him, he).
5. Scrooge sees the ghost but doesn't want to believe (it, them).
6. His dead partner warns (him, he) that he has to change his ways.
7. The ghost of Christmas Past arrives, and Scrooge goes with (she, it) to his youth.
8. The ghost of Christmas Present shows (he, him) his less fortunate clerk's family.
9. Scrooge watches (him, them) celebrate Christmas, even though they are poor.
10. The ghost of Christmas Future presents (he, him) with the shadows of what may yet come.
11. When he wakes up, Scrooge goes to the clerk's family and brings presents and food to (her, them) because, as he says, "The spirits have changed (I, me)."
12. Every year people tell this story; it reminds (they, them) about their responsibility to help their neighbors.

B. Choosing Object Pronouns

Fill in the blanks in the following sentences with appropriate object pronouns. Vary the pronouns you use, and do not use the pronoun *you*.

1. That much exercise really tires ______________.
2. Tell ______________ about your recent good fortune.
3. The tour guide showed ______________ around the White House.
4. My brother gave ______________ his binoculars.
5. We grilled hamburgers for ______________.
6. Are you going with ______________ to the recycling center?
7. Remind ______________ that we are eating dinner early.

Name ______________________________ Date ______________

Lesson 3

Object Pronouns

Application

A. Proofreading

The following story contains several errors in the use of object pronouns. When you find a pronoun used incorrectly, cross it out. Then insert this proofreading symbol ⌃ and write the correct pronoun above it.

Charles Dickens wrote *Great Expectations,* the story of a poor boy named Pip. One day Miss Havisham, a strange, rich woman, calls he to her house. She takes care of a beautiful girl named Estella, and she wants Pip to play with she. He visits them throughout his childhood. However, they don't treat him very well. Surprisingly, when Pip becomes old enough, he inherits a great deal of money. Because Miss Havisham is the only rich person he knows, he assumes the money came from she. He becomes a proper gentleman in London, and the rest of the book shows he in his new lifestyle. Later, he learns that his money came from an escaped convict he helped when he was younger. Pip had helped the convict only because he had been afraid of he. Read the classic story to find out what happens next.

B. Using Object Pronouns in Writing

Think about a character, real or fictional, whom you admire. How does that person show the qualities you admire most? Write a short description of a real or imaginary meeting with him or her. Use at least four object pronouns in your paragraph.

CHAPTER 3

Name ______________________ Date ____________

Lesson 4

Possessive Pronouns

Teaching

Possessive pronouns are personal pronouns used to show ownership or relationship.

Possessive Pronouns

Singular	Plural
my, mine	our, ours
your, yours	your, yours
her, hers, his, its	their, theirs

The possessive pronouns *my, your, her, his, our,* and *their* come before nouns. The possessive pronouns *mine, ours, yours, his, hers,* and *theirs* can stand alone in a sentence.

> My tennis serve is powerful but not very accurate.
> My teammate's legs are stiff and sore from running, but mine feel fine.

CHAPTER 3

Some possessive pronouns sound like contractions *(its/it's, your/you're, their/they're).* Don't confuse these pairs. Remember that possessive pronouns never use an apostrophe. Contractions always use an apostrophe.

> Contraction You're never going to hit his fastball.
> Possessive Your fastball is hard to hit, but his is impossible.

A.Identifying Possessive Pronouns

Underline all the possessive pronouns in the following sentences.

1. The athletes at our school should be proud of their performances this year.
2. Her backstroke is improving, and she really excels in the butterfly.
3. They had to win this game so their team could go to the state championships.
4. Cross-country was our school's best athletic event.
5. When he hit the golf ball, he could see its flight was heading straight to the hole.
6. They had worked hard to earn the trophy, and now the glory was theirs.

B. Using Possessive Pronouns

Underline the correct pronoun to complete each sentence.

1. (Their, they're) dedication to the game could be seen in how well they played.
2. Even the judges were amazed at (her, hers) performance in the gymnastics competition.
3. Public speaking was not (his, its) best talent, but he did well on the debate team.
4. John's track meet last year was a disaster. (Your, Yours) turned out much better.
5. The basketball team had a tough year, but (its, it's) hopes are high for next year.
6. Those cheerleaders are gymnasts too. (Your, You're) cheerleaders could learn some routines from them.
7. When (they're, their) scores were posted, the athletes cheered.

Name ______________________________ Date ______________

Lesson 4

Possessive Pronouns

More Practice

A. Using Possessive Pronouns

In each sentence, underline the pronoun that completes each sentence correctly.

1. Someone should have tried to block (her, its) shot. It was the game winner!
2. Lewis found the chess meet to be tougher than (his, its) football game.
3. It was (my, mine) proudest moment when I won the diving competition.
4. (Your, You're) football team should score a lot of points this year.
5. You can give up or try harder. It's (you're, your) choice.
6. The runners dropped the baton in the 800-meter relay. (It's, Its) handle was too slippery.
7. When we fumbled on the five-yard line, we suddenly knew that victory was (their, theirs).
8. The news article said that it was (her, hers) determination that made Kelly into a world-class skier.
9. Has the principal seen the students' petition? They want (they're, their) school to have a speed skating team.
10. No one who watched Kevin play golf could believe (his, its) luck in sinking that 40-foot putt.
11. Paula had worked hard, and everyone expected (her, hers) project to win first prize at the science fair.

CHAPTER 3

B. Choosing Possessive Pronouns

Fill in the blanks in the following sentences with appropriate possessive pronouns. Vary the pronouns you use.

1. The theater gave free passes to ________________ staff.
2. ________________ idea for the experiment might work.
3. They are picking up ________________ uniforms now.
4. Have you made up ________________ mind about going?
5. Are these your gym shoes or ________________?
6. His voice carries farther than ________________.
7. After the game, the twins asked us over to ________________ house.

Name ______________________________ Date ______________

Lesson 4

Possessive Pronouns

Application

A. Proofreading

Proofread the following story to make sure that possessive pronouns have been used in the right places. When you find a pronoun used incorrectly, cross it out. Then insert this proofreading symbol ^ and write the correct pronoun above it.

This was probably the biggest weekend in they're school's history. Jennifer knew it was the biggest weekend of her life. The baseball team was playing it's semifinal games on Saturday. If they won, their players would go to the regional playoffs. "My brother's pitching, and your is catching," she said to her friend Aya on the phone. "I wish we could be there." Jennifer and Aya had their own competition to attend. They were both on the varsity track team, and its final meet of the season was also on Saturday. "I really hope we win," said Aya. "I know you'll do your best, and I'll do my." Another big event would happen on Sunday. "I can't believe you're sister is performing in the national finals for piano," Jennifer remarked to Aya. "What a weekend!"

CHAPTER 3

B. Using Possessive Pronouns in Writing

Write a letter to an athlete you admire. Tell him or her the reasons for your admiration by pointing out what you like best about how he or she plays or lives life. Use at least five possessive pronouns in your paragraph.

Name ______________________________ Date ______________

Lesson 5

Reflexive and Intensive Pronouns

Teaching

Pronouns that end in *-self* or *-selves* are either **reflexive** or **intensive** pronouns.

Reflexive and Intensive Pronouns		
myself	yourself	herself, himself, itself
ourselves	yourselves	themselves

A **reflexive pronoun** refers to the subject and directs the action of the verb back to the subject. Reflexive pronouns are necessary to the meaning of a sentence. Without them the sentence doesn't make sense.

> Explorers cannot stop <u>themselves</u> from taking chances. (*Themselves* refers to *explorers.*)

An **intensive pronoun** emphasizes the noun or pronoun within the same sentence. Intensive pronouns are not necessary to the meaning of the sentence.

> The queen <u>herself</u> asked Ponce de León to find the fountain of youth. (*Herself* refers to *the queen.*)

Remember that *hisself* and *theirselves* are not real words. Never use them. Use *himself* and *themselves* instead.

CHAPTER 3

A. Identifying Reflexive and Intensive Pronouns

Underline all the reflexive and intensive pronouns in the following sentences.

1. Juan Ponce de León had heard tales of a fountain of youth and wanted to find it for himself.
2. The fountain of youth itself was said to be located on an island called Bimini in the Bahamas.
3. It is possible that the Native Americans themselves believed that the fountain of youth existed.
4. Supposedly, if you drank the fountain water, you would find yourself restored to youth.
5. Do you yourself believe that a fountain of youth exists somewhere?

B. Using Reflexive and Intensive Pronouns

Underline the correct pronoun to complete each sentence.

1. Although Ferdinand Magellan (him, himself) did not live to complete the journey, he led the first expedition to sail around the world.
2. Unbelievably, only 18 crewmen out of the 250 who began the difficult trip were able to bring (theirselves, themselves) back home safely.
3. On an island in the Pacific, the crew found (themselves, them) in a bloody war.
4. In fact, Magellan (hisself, himself) was killed in a battle on the island.
5. Do you ever ask (you, yourself) whether you could have been an explorer?

Name ______________________________ Date ______________

Lesson 5

Reflexive and Intensive Pronouns

More Practice

A. Recognizing Reflexive and Intensive Pronouns

Underline the reflexive or intensive pronoun in each sentence. On the line, write **R** if the pronoun is reflexive and **I** if it is intensive.

1. Have you yourself ever traveled to Africa? ______

2. Mary Henrietta Kingsley made three journeys to West Africa all by herself, becoming the first European to visit some parts of Africa. ______

3. Many people considered it improper for a woman to travel alone, and Kingsley was forced to explain herself over and over again. ______

4. On a journey like this one, you can find yourself in many difficult situations. ______

5. Travelers themselves must think of ways to survive. ______

6. Africans themselves could not quite understand this outspoken young woman. ______

7. Kingsley put herself in danger again when she tended wounded soldiers during the Boer War. ______

8. There, this adventurer put aside her own dreams of travel and helped soldiers who could not help themselves. ______

CHAPTER 3

B. Choosing Reflexive and Intensive Pronouns

Fill in the blanks in the following sentences with appropriate reflexive or intensive pronouns. On the line to the right, write **R** for reflexive or **I** for intensive.

1. The doctor ________________ came out to greet her patients. ______

2. Steve accompanies ________________ on the guitar. ______

3. Terry, repeat to ________________ those words of encouragement. ______

4. The movie ________________ was boring, but the cartoon was hilarious. ______

5. We churned butter ________________ when we lived on the farm. ______

6. Carol taught ________________ how to play the piano. ______

Name ______________________________ Date ______________

Lesson 5

Reflexive and Intensive Pronouns

Application

A. Proofreading

Proofread the following story to make sure that reflexive and intensive pronouns have been used correctly. When you find a pronoun used incorrectly, cross it out. Then insert this proofreading symbol ^ and write the correct pronoun above it.

Have you ever heard of Marco Polo? He hisself, along with his father and uncle, was one of the first Europeans to travel into China. His father and uncle were theirselves great travelers. These two Venetian merchants had traveled from Italy all the way to China. They brought home fascinating stories about foreign customs and treasures. The next time they went, they brought young Marco with them. The Mongol ruler of China hisself, Kublai Kahn, became their host. Marco spent 17 years traveling around China by himself. Later, Marco entertained the khan by telling stories about what he had seen and done. His travel accounts were recorded in a journal, although it is possible he didn't write it hisself. Reading Marco Polo's journal theirselves, Europeans got an exciting glimpse into a different world. Today, when we see the world becoming closer and more connected, we should remind us that at one time, few people traveled far from their homes.

B. Using Reflexive and Intensive Pronouns in Writing

Everyone has lost an important item at one time or another. Tell about a time when you or someone you know searched high and low for something lost. Use at least four reflexive or intensive pronouns in your story.

CHAPTER 3

Name ______________________________ Date ______________

Lesson 6 Interrogatives and Demonstratives

Teaching

An **interrogative pronoun** is used to introduce a question. The interrogative pronouns are *who, whom, what, which,* and *whose.*

Who is always used as a subject or a predicate pronoun.

Subject	Who has the suntan lotion?
Predicate pronoun	The lifeguard is who?

Whom is always used as an object.

Direct object	Whom did the lifeguard rescue?
Indirect object	He gave whom a lecture about safety?
Object of preposition	With whom will you walk on the beach?

Don't confuse *whose* with *who's. Who* is a contraction that means *who is.*

Who's the fastest swimmer?
Whose are these sandals?

CHAPTER 3

A **demonstrative pronoun** points out a person, place, thing, or idea. The demonstrative pronouns—*this, that, these,* and *those*—are used alone in a sentence. Never use *here* or *there* with a demonstrative pronoun.

Singular	This is our blanket. That is yours.
Plural	These are your waterwings. Those are hers.

A. Using Interrogative Pronouns

Underline the pronoun that correctly completes each sentence.

1. (Who, Whom) will the choir director choose?
2. The winner was (who, whom)?
3. (Who, Whom) discovered the valuable Hope Diamond?
4. The mail carrier brought (who, whom) that big package?
5. For (who, whom) was the house built?
6. (Who, Whom) makes the best apple strudel?
7. (Whose, Who's) are these mittens?

B. Using Demonstrative Pronouns

Underline the correct pronoun to complete each sentence.

1. (That, Those) are the rules of the game.
2. (This, These) are the kinds of mistakes that I keep making.
3. (This here, This) is the second day in a row of record-breaking heat.
4. For all I know, (that, that there) might have been your last chance.
5. Give (these, these here) a try; I think you'll like them.
6. I can see the titles of these paintings, but I can't see the titles on (those, those there).

Name ______________________________ Date ______________

Lesson 6

Interrogatives and Demonstratives

More Practice

A. Using Interrogative Pronouns

In each sentence, underline the pronoun that completes each sentence correctly.

1. The director chose (whom, who) for the role?
2. (Who, Whom) was the 16th president of the United States?
3. For (who, whom) was the message intended?
4. (Who's, Whose) are these notebooks?
5. (Who, Whom) wrote the play *Driving Miss Daisy?*
6. By (whom, who) was the mural painted?
7. (Who, Whom) supplied the refreshments for the dance?
8. (Who's, Whose) is this tape recorder?
9. Your favorite quarterback is (who, whom)?
10. (Who's, Whose) is the scarf on the top shelf?
11. (Who, Whom) are the people in the photograph?
12. For (who, whom) are we waiting?

CHAPTER 3

B. Choosing Demonstrative Pronouns

Fill in the blanks in the following sentences with appropriate demonstrative pronouns.

1. ______________ was a very nice thing to do.

2. ______________ are the movies that always give me bad dreams.

3. ______________ are Julie's earrings here on the dresser.

4. Arrange ______________ in a vase, please.

5. ______________ is our school, across the field.

6. ______________ on the shelf are my sister's CDs.

7. ______________ is my homework assignment for tomorrow.

8. ______________ are the newest books from the library.

9. ______________ is my baseball card collection.

10. Mom told us to pick tomatoes, but ______________ aren't ripe yet.

11. May I see your sketches? ______________ are mine.

12. I want a comfortable chair, and ______________ seems perfect.

Name ______________________ Date ______________

Lesson 6

Interrogatives and Demonstratives

Application

A. Writing Sentences with Interrogative Pronouns

Write a question to go with each of these answers. Use the interrogative pronoun *who, whom,* or *whose* in each question.

EXAMPLE Answer: *Who rang the bell?*
Question: Nicole rang the bell.

1. Question: ______________________

Answer: Our next-door neighbor is Mr. Kolar.

2. Question: ______________________

Answer: The plants on the roof are his.

3. Question: ______________________

Answer: Mr. O'Connor baked the cookies for his grandchildren.

4. Question: ______________________

Answer: I will e-mail my friend Colin.

5. Question: ______________________

Answer: Colin gave his e-mail address to me.

B. Using Pronouns in Writing

Imagine that you are a detective investigating the theft of an expensive pair of sneakers. Write five questions you would ask suspects and witnesses. Use one of the interrogative pronouns *who, whom,* or *whose* in each question.

1. ______________________

____

2. ______________________

____

3. ______________________

____

4. ______________________

____

5. ______________________

____

Name ______________________ Date ______________

Lesson 7

Pronoun-Antecedent Agreement

Teaching

The **antecedent** is the noun or pronoun that a pronoun refers to or replaces. Pronouns must agree with their antecedents in number, person, and gender.

Number Use a singular pronoun to refer to a singular antecedent. Use a plural pronoun to refer to a plural antecedent.

Settlers moved to the American West and found that it was a huge and wild land.
When the settlers got together, they told stories with huge and wild heroes.

Person The **person** (first person, second person, third person) of a pronoun must be the same as the person of the antecedent. Avoid switching from one person to another in the same sentence or paragraph.

First Person We read tall tales that are a part of our American heritage.
Second Person You can make up your own tall tale.

Third Person The students shared their stories.

Gender The **gender** of a pronoun must be the same as the gender of its antecedent. Personal pronouns have three gender forms: masculine *(he, him, his)*, feminine *(she, her, hers)*, and neuter *(it, its)*. Don't use only masculine or feminine pronouns when you mean to refer to both genders.

Marlene told her story to the class.
Haydon drew pictures to accompany his tall tale.
Each student had his or her favorite story.

CHAPTER 3

Identifying Pronouns and Their Antecedents

In each sentence, underline the personal pronoun once and its antecedent twice.

1. Some tall tales are about real people, but the stories about them are exaggerated.
2. Other characters in tall tales are imaginary, but they are fascinating!
3. For example, steel-drivin' man John Henry challenged a steam drill to a contest and beat it.
4. Johnny Appleseed planted apple seeds with the hope they would sprout, grow, and provide fruit for new settlers.
5. Everyone remembers Sweet Betsy from Pike and her travels across the wide prairie.
6. Davy Crockett bragged that he was half horse, half alligator.
7. Slaves, yearning for freedom, told stories of a time when they could fly.
8. The stories about Mike Fink tell of his life as King of the Keelboatmen, the men who worked on cargo boats on the Mississippi River.
9. Sally Ann Thunder Ann Whirlwind claimed she could defeat a grizzly bear and make a lasso out of six rattlesnakes.
10. And who could forget giant lumberjack Paul Bunyan and his companion, Babe the Blue Ox?

Name ______________________________ Date ______________

Lesson 7 Pronoun-Antecedent Agreement *More Practice*

A. Identifying Pronouns and Their Antecedents

In each sentence, draw an arrow to connect each pronoun to its antecedent.

1. Stories about Pecos Bill claim that he was America's greatest cowboy.
2. Old coyotes can remember when Bill was little and lived with them.
3. Bill tamed a wild mustang and named him Widow-Maker.
4. Some people say that Bill once caught a cyclone and rode it around the country.
5. Bill finally married. His bride's name was Slue-Foot Sue.
6. When Bill met Sue, she was riding a catfish as big as a whale.
7. Stories say that Bill died laughing when he tried to answer a city slicker's foolish questions about cowpunching.

CHAPTER 3

B. Making Pronouns and Antecedents Agree

Write a pronoun that correctly completes each sentence. Then underline the antecedent of the pronoun.

1. A spotted coat helps the leopard hide from ______________ prey.
2. Snow covered the ballpark earlier, but ______________ melted.
3. Ken came by and picked up ______________ baseball before supper.
4. Many artists build ______________ studios in old warehouses.
5. Greta could help if ______________ set the table for dinner.
6. Silicon is important because ______________ is used to make computer chips.
7. Jay opened the envelope, and ______________ found nothing in it.
8. The brothers wanted to buy a stereo, but it was too expensive for ______________.
9. Manuel's friends love to ski; ______________ go skiing often.
10. Paul lent Sandi ______________ bicycle because hers was broken.

Name ______________________ Date ______________

Lesson 7

Pronoun-Antecedent Agreement

Application

A. Making Pronouns and Antecedents Agree in Writing

Read the following paragraph. Look especially for errors in agreement between pronouns and their antecedents. On the lines below, write the numbers of the sentences with agreement errors. Then write each of those sentences correctly.

(1) When loggers got together on winter evenings, they often talked about the biggest lumberjack of all, Paul Bunyan. **(2)** Shortly after Paul was born, it weighed 80 pounds. **(3)** It was so big, he knocked down a mile of trees just by rolling over in their sleep. **(4)** Her parents used a wagon pulled by a team of oxen as its baby carriage. **(5)** Years later, Paul rescued Babe, the Blue Ox, and they were never apart. **(6)** She worked cutting down trees, and Babe pulled it to the sawmill. **(7)** Paul hired many men to work with him. **(8)** The men liked working with Paul because he made sure she always had enough to eat. **(9)** Paul's cook made pancakes on a griddle so large that 50 men with bacon slabs tied to its feet skated around the griddle to grease him. **(10)** They were glad the cook made stacks of pancakes for them.

____

____

____

____

____

____

____

____

B. Writing with Pronouns

On the lines below, rewrite a familiar folktale or write an original tall tale. If you write a tall tale, use plenty of imagination and exaggeration. Be sure to include at least four personal pronouns with clear antecedents in your story.

____

____

____

____

____

____

CHAPTER 3

Name ______________________ Date ____________

Lesson 8 Indefinite Pronoun Agreement

Teaching

An **indefinite pronoun** does not refer to a specific person, place, thing, or idea. Indefinite pronouns often do not have antecedents.

Indefinite pronouns can be singular, plural, or either singular or plural.

Indefinite Pronouns

Singular				Plural	Singular or Plural	
another	each	everything	one	both	all	none
anybody	either	neither	somebody	few	any	some
anyone	everybody	nobody	someone	many	most	
anything	everyone	no one	something	several		

Use a singular personal pronoun to refer to a singular indefinite pronoun. Use *his or her* when the antecedent could be either masculine or feminine.

Everyone turned his or her eyes to Cape Canaveral for the liftoff.

Use a plural personal pronoun to refer to a plural indefinite pronoun.

Several of the witnesses covered their eyes in fear.

Some indefinite pronouns can be singular or plural. Often, the phrase that follows the indefinite pronoun tells you whether the indefinite pronoun is singular or plural.

All of the flight went according to its schedule. (singular)

All of the flights went according to their schedules. (plural)

Using Indefinite Pronouns

In each sentence, underline the correct pronoun choice.

1. All of the astronauts take (his or her, their) training seriously.
2. Each of the program instructors is expert in (his or her, their) specialty.
3. Everybody in the space program was chosen for (their, his or her) abilities.
4. Many are eager for (their, his or her) chance to prove they have the right stuff.
5. Each of the astronauts should know how to handle (his or her, their) ship in case of trouble.
6. Both of the first astronauts accepted (his, their) country's gratitude.
7. Neither of the astronauts was ashamed of (his, their) performance.
8. Someone waved (his or her, their) gloved hand to the crowd and then stepped aboard the space shuttle.
9. Some missions of the space program have had (its, their) share of tragedies.
10. Everyone alive during the explosion of the *Challenger* remembers how (he or she, they) heard the terrible news.
11. All of Christa MacAuliffe's students remember (his or her, their) teacher with gratitude and admiration.

Name ______________________________ Date ______________

Lesson 8

Indefinite Pronoun Agreement

More Practice

A. Identifying Indefinite Pronouns

Underline the indefinite pronoun in each sentence. Then underline the correct pronoun in parentheses.

1. Many of Rembrandt's paintings have lost (its, their) original colors.
2. Each of the boys prepared (his, their) report independently.
3. All of the salespeople sold (his or her, their) goods at the convention.
4. Nobody expects to hear (his or her, their) name on the radio.
5. If anyone wants to be a doctor, tell (him or her, them) to volunteer for hospital work.
6. Neither of the cats had (its, their) nails clipped.
7. Everyone had a chance to state (his or her, their) opinions.
8. None of the medicine was labeled with (their, its) expiration date.
9. Anyone in the choir can bring (his or her, their) family to the concert.
10. Somebody has left (his or her, their) wallet on my desk.
11. Many of the rescue workers wore (his or her, their) own safety gear.
12. The skaters were choosy; several insisted on selecting the music for (his or her, their) programs.

CHAPTER 3

B. Using Pronouns Correctly

In each sentence below, decide whether the pronouns agree with their antecedents. If the sentence is correct, write **Correct** on the line. If it contains a pronoun that does not agree with its antecedent, rewrite the sentence correctly on the line.

1. Everyone was glued to the television set after they heard the news.

____

2. Some of the networks changed its programming.

____

3. Everyone was shocked by what they had heard.

____

4. Most of the witnesses couldn't believe their eyes.

____

5. Nobody who saw the explosion could get it out of their mind.

____

Name ________________________________ Date ______________

Lesson 8

Indefinite Pronoun Agreement

Application

A. Proofreading for Indefinite Pronoun Agreement

Proofread the following paragraph. When you find pronoun-antecedent error, cross out the pronoun. Then insert this proofreading symbol ^ and write the correct pronoun or pronouns above it.

How would you like to be an astronaut? Everybody, even an astronaut in space, must take care of their body. Without healthy bodies, people can't function at peak level. To make sure the astronauts stay healthy, the space program has provided them with some basic necessities. None of the astronauts' food (some of which comes from a tube) tastes as good as their counterpart on Earth, but dietitians have made them nutritious and easy to eat. All of the astronauts need his or her sleep time. For that reason, each of the astronauts has their own sleeping couch. This couch is probably not too comfortable, and an astronaut has to strap himself or herself to it to keep from floating away. Could you stand these conditions for weeks? The sad truth is that even though almost everyone dreams about the adventure of space travel, they may not have the willpower to face its uncomfortable realities.

B. Using Indefinite Pronouns in Writing

Imagine that you are one of six astronauts aboard a space shuttle. Write a diary entry about part of a day in space. Tell what you did and what others in your group did and said. Use at least four indefinite pronouns. Be sure that any personal pronouns agree with their indefinite pronoun antecedents in number.

CHAPTER 3

Name ______________________________ Date ______________

Lesson 9

Pronoun Problems

Teaching

We and *Us* with Nouns

The pronouns *we* and *us* are often followed by a noun that identifies the pronoun (*we workers, us workers*).

Use *we* when the noun is a subject or a predicate noun. Use *us* when the noun is an object.

We workers were tired after the job. (*We* were tired.)
The supervisor gave us workers a break. (The supervisor gave *us* the break.)

Unclear Reference

Be sure that each personal pronoun refers clearly to only one person, place, or thing.

Confusing Laurie and Susan care about the environment. She has volunteered to clean up the park. (Who has volunteered?)

Clear Laurie and Susan care about the environment. Laurie has volunteered to clean up the park.

A. Choosing the Correct Pronoun

In each sentence, underline the correct pronoun form.

1. (We, Us) visitors paid five dollars to enter the old house.
2. The price increase is not popular with (we, us) comic book readers.
3. (We, Us) artists are showing our work at the school.
4. Mrs. Watson chose (we, us) eighth graders to be library aides.
5. If (we, us) quilters get together, we can make a beautiful quilt.
6. The city requires (we, us) dog owners to keep our dogs on leashes.
7. To (we, us) experienced climbers, this climb was quite easy.
8. (We, Us) marchers waved to the crowds on the sidewalk.

B. Avoiding Unclear Reference

In each set, circle the letter of the sentence that is stated more clearly.

1. **a.** Kim and Rita take long walks every day, but Kim walks farther than Rita.
   b. Kim and Rita take long walks every day, but she walks farther than she.
2. **a.** Lewis is bringing both running shoes and sandals. He says they look better, but they feel better.
   b. Lewis is bringing both running shoes and sandals. He says the sandals look better, but the running shoes feel better.
3. **a.** Joann and Georgia wear glasses. She is getting contact lenses.
   b. Joann and Georgia wear glasses. Georgia is getting contact lenses.

CHAPTER 3

Name ______________________ Date ____________

Lesson 9

Pronoun Problems

More Practice

A. Choosing the Correct Pronoun

In each sentence, underline the correct pronoun form.

1. (Us, We) volunteers were happy to see the park looking good again.

2. Are (we, us) students invited to the concert?

3. Just as (we, us) campers got our tents up, it started to rain.

4. (We, Us) doctors are concerned about the possibility of infection.

5. The pool is open to (we, us) swimmers after 10 o'clock.

6. The driver announced each bus stop to (we, us) passengers.

7. Mom met (we, us) travelers at the airport gate.

8. The bill's supporters are contacting (we, us) voters.

9. The most worried people in the world were (we, us) suspects.

10. (We, Us) learners all take in information in different ways.

CHAPTER 3

B. Avoiding Unclear Reference

Rewrite each of these sentences to make them clear.

1. When Justin and Tony watch TV together, he refuses to share the remote.

____

2. Both Susan B. Anthony and Elizabeth Cady Stanton were active in the women's rights movement, but most people remember only her.

____

3. Miko and Anne are interested in travel. She and her family are going to Japan this summer.

____

4. The van and the truck reached the intersection at the same time, but it pulled away more quickly.

____

5. Carol and Tracy went to the restaurant, and she ordered a chef's salad.

____

6. Whenever Simon and Brad get into an argument, he always apologizes first.

____

Name ______________________ Date ____________

Lesson 9

Pronoun Problems

Application

A. Using Pronouns Correctly

Use each of the phrases printed below in an original sentence.

EXAMPLE we bicyclists
We bicyclists signaled a left turn.

1. we gardeners ______________________

2. us guests ______________________

3. us customers ______________________

4. we boaters ______________________

CHAPTER 3

B. Proofreading for Correct Pronoun Usage

The following paragraph is filled with unclear references. Rewrite the paragraph more clearly on the lines below.

Alfonso and Ed are doing a report on immigration into the United States during the early 20th century. In doing his research, he found some interesting information about Ellis Island. Many of them passed through the station on Ellis Island on their way into the United States. Then he found some photographs of Ellis Island and the immigrants who stopped there. Alfonso and Ed were both excited about the immigrant journals they found. He decided to work with him to make a slide show. He would read the words of the immigrants as the pictures were shown on the screen. Maybe he could find more photographs for the slide show. Both the boys set to work looking for more photos and more information about the immigrant experience.

Name ______________________ Date ______________

Lesson 10

More Pronoun Problems

Teaching

Using Pronouns in Compounds Use the subject pronouns *I, she, he, we* and *they* in a compound subject or with a predicate noun or pronoun. Use the object pronouns *me, her, him, us,* and *them* in a compound object.

Compound subject	Marie and he performed experiments.
Compound predicate pronoun	Amazing scientists were Pierre and she.
Compound object	They awarded Marie and him the Nobel Prize.

Phrases That Interfere Sometimes words and phrases come between a subject and a pronoun that refers to it. Be sure the pronoun agrees with the subject.

Marie Curie, unlike today's scientists, didn't understand the risk she was taking.

(*She* refers to *Marie Curie.*)

A. Using Pronouns in Compounds

Underline the pronoun that completes each sentence correctly.

1. Marya Sklodowska was a brilliant science student in 1891 when she met Pierre Curie. Marya and (him, he) fell in love and were married in 1895.

2. Great researchers were Pierre and (she, her).

3. The search for radioactive elements fascinated Marya, now known as Marie, and (he, him).

4. Pierre and (her, she) knew that uranium gave off strange rays.

5. It seemed possible to Pierre and (her, she) that other elements could do the same.

6. After many experiments, Marie and (he, him) discovered a radioactive element they called radium.

7. Too bad they didn't know the harm it was causing Pierre and (she, her).

8. In 1903, Marie and (he, him) won the Nobel Prize in physics.

9. But radiation poisoning was already affecting Pierre and (her, she).

B. Dealing with Phrases That Interfere

Draw arrows from the boldfaced pronouns to the words they modify.

1. Pierre, who sometimes took radium from his pocket to show his friends, discovered that **his** health was failing.

2. The muscles all over his body were losing **their** tone.

3. His skin, which had touched radium for years, looked as if **it** had been burned.

4. Pierre, greatly weakened by the disease, lost **his** life when he stepped in front of an oncoming cart.

CHAPTER 3

Name ______________________ Date ______________

Lesson 10

More Pronoun Problems

More Practice

A. Using Pronouns in Compounds

Underline the pronoun that completes each sentence correctly.

1. Were you and (they, them) the winners?

2. The teacher called on Stan and (her, she).

3. Between you and (I, me), I didn't really understand that joke.

4. (He, Him) and I are working on a science project.

5. Lily and (I, me) drew the cartoons for the newspaper.

6. A taxi is taking (they, them) and us to the airport.

7. The Jaspers and (she, her) are good friends.

8. Rosita borrowed the CD from my brother and (me, I).

9. The best dancers were Mimi and (him, he).

10. Will you drive the Breens and (we, us) to school)?

B. Dealing with Phrases That Interfere

Decide if the pronouns in each sentence are used correctly. If the sentence has an error, rewrite the sentence on the line. If the sentence is written correctly, write **Correct** on the line.

1. The Curies, both great people of science, were ahead of its time.

____

2. Radium, with its radioactive rays, was more dangerous than the Curies thought they could be.

____

____

3. The shed they worked in was famous for its leaks and drafts.

____

4. Marie, unaware of the danger of radium, kept some of them by her bed so she could see by its constant light.

____

____

5. Marie, an excellent student in physics, earned their doctorate in 1903.

____

Name ________________________________ Date ______________

Lesson 10

More Pronoun Problems

Application

A. Proofreading

Proofread this paragraph. Look especially for errors in the use of pronouns. When you find an error, cross out the pronoun used incorrectly. Insert this symbol ^ and write the correct pronoun above it.

One of the most famous teams in the history of science was Marie and Pierre Curie. To he and she we owe much of our understanding of radioactivity. For that knowledge, they sacrificed their lives. Marie and him spent countless hours in a drafty shed doing experiments. They were looking for an element that would give off radioactive rays. To Pierre and her, the search was fascinating. Once Pierre and her found the element radium, Marie was able to write about her findings and earn her doctorate. However, radium took its toll on the health of Pierre and she. They did not know that this element was dangerous, so Marie and him handled it freely, without even using gloves. Pierre and she both eventually died of radiation poisoning.

CHAPTER 3

B. Making Pronouns Agree with Their Antecedents

Below are the beginnings of several sentences. Each beginning contains the sentence's subject. For each sentence beginning, choose an ending from the list below. Write your ending on the line.

EXAMPLE Pierre enjoyed showing radium to *his friends*.

his chemicals	his friends
their prize	their work
her doctorate	its damage

1. The scientists, with great determination, continued ________________.
2. Marie, unlike many other women during those years, wanted to earn ________________.
3. Pierre, a teacher, didn't have enough money to pay for ________________.
4. The Curies, after years of work, were proud of ________________.
5. Radium, one of the most dangerous substances on Earth, finally did ________________ and killed Marie when she was 66 years old.

Name ______________________ Date ____________

Lesson 1 What Is a Verb?

Teaching

A **verb** is a word used to express an action, a condition, or a state of being. The two main kinds of verbs are action verbs and linking verbs. Both kinds can be appear with helping verbs

An **action verb** tells what the subject does. The action may be physical or mental.

She **rides** motorcycles. (physical action) I **prefer** a bike. (mental action)

A **linking verb** links the subject of the sentence to a word in the predicate. The most common linking verbs are forms of the verb *be,* as in *We **are** late.*

Linking Verbs	Sample Verbs
Forms of be	be, is, am, are, was, were, been, being
Verbs that express condition	look, smell, feel, sound, taste, grow, appear, become, seem

Some verbs may act either as action verbs or as linking verbs.

She **smells** the perfume. (action) It **smells** flowery. (linking)

Helping verbs help the main verb express action or show time. They are combined with the main verbs to form verb phrases.

He **has planted** the crops. (The helping verb is **has.** The main verb is **planted.**)

A few verbs can serve as either helping verbs or main verbs.

He **has** a tractor. (The main verb is **has.**)

Common Helping Verbs	
Forms of *have:* has, have, had	**Forms of be:** be, am, is, are, was, were, been, being
Forms of *do:* do, does, did	**Others:** could, should, would, may, might, must, can, shall, will

CHAPTER 4

Identifying Verbs

Underline the verb or verb phrase in each sentence. On the line to the right, label the verb with **A** for action or **L** for linking.

1. The subway travels at fast speeds under the ground. ______

2. During rush hour, the subway trains become quite crowded. ______

3. The subway driver controls the trains. ______

4. Some subways are over the ground. ______

5. The trains stay on their train tracks at all times. ______

6. Subways cause less air pollution than do automobiles. ______

7. However, subways sound very loud to nearby onlookers. ______

8. I ride the subway often. ______

Name ______________________________ Date ______________

Lesson 1

What Is a Verb?

More Practice

A. Identifying Verbs

Underline the verb or verb phrase in each sentence. On the line to the right, label the verb with **A** for action or **L** for linking.

1. Mail travels overseas on airplanes. _____
2. Mail also can go overseas by boats. _____
3. Boats are slower but less expensive. _____
4. Most people send their mail overseas by airplane. _____
5. Boats might take weeks for the trip across the ocean. _____
6. Boats were once the only form of transportation across the ocean. _____
7. The post office can use trucks, trains, and planes to move mail. _____
8. In the past, horses have carried mail across the country. _____

B. Identifying Helping Verbs and Main Verbs

In Exercise A, find four sentences that use helping verbs. In each box below, write those sentence numbers and the parts of each verb phrase in the correct columns.

Helping Verb(s)	Main Verb	Helping Verb(s)	Main Verb
#___ ________	________	#___ ________	________
#___ ________	________	#___ ________	________

CHAPTER 4

C. Using Verbs

In each sentence, replace the underlined verb with a more specific verb.

1. A hovercraft <u>stays</u> above the water surface on a layer of blown air.

   ____

2. Jumbo jets <u>move</u> at speeds of 550 miles per hour.

   ____

3. Animals, such as horses and camels, <u>get</u> people and goods over the land.

   ____

4. Robert Fulton <u>made</u> the first efficient steamboat, the *Clermont.*

   ____

Name ______________________________ Date ______________

Lesson 1

What Is a Verb?

Application

A. Identifying and Replacing Verbs

In each sentence, underline the verb or verb phrase. If the verb is an action verb, rewrite the sentence with another action verb. If the original verb is a linking verb, simply write **Linking.**

1. The Alaskan pipeline transports over two million barrels of oil per day.

____

2. Automobiles are the most popular mode of transportation today.

____

3. Europeans use trains more often than Americans do.

____

4. The rotation of rotor blades moves a helicopter.

____

5. All passengers in cars should wear their seat belts.

____

6. A tow truck has moved the broken-down car.

____

CHAPTER 4

B. Using Verbs

On each line, write an action verb that makes sense in the sentence and paragraph. Underline every linking verb.

My uncle travels across the country often. He ______________ different modes of transportation. He ______________ his car sometimes, but only in good weather. Also, he ______________ cars when he doesn't want to put too many miles on his own car. Often he ______________ on airplanes for the longer journeys. However, for variety he ______________ a ticket for the train. It's a more entertaining way to travel than the plane. Next time, he says, he will ______________ either by boat or by helicopter.

Name ______________________ Date ______________

Lesson 2

Action Verbs and Objects

Teaching

Action verbs often require words that complete their meaning. These words are called **complements.** These complements are direct objects and indirect objects.

A **direct object** is a word or words that name the receiver of the action. It answers *what* or *whom* receives the action of the verb.

> Larry tells **stories.** (*What* does Larry tell? *stories*)

An **indirect object** tells *to what* or *whom* or *for what* or *whom* an action is done. Verbs that take indirect objects include *bring, give, make, send, show, teach, tell,* and *write.*

> Larry tells **his friends** stories. (*To whom* does Larry tell stories? *his friends*)

Remember that if the preposition to appears before a word, that word is not an indirect object.

Transitive and Intransitive Verbs An action verb that has a direct object is called a **transitive verb.** An action verb that does not have a direct object is an **intransitive verb.**

Do not be confused when an intransitive verb is followed by an adverb. A direct object tells *what* or *whom,* while an adverb tells *how, when, where,* or *to what extent.*

> Gina **claps** her hands. (*What* does Gina clap? *hands* Here ***claps*** is transitive.)
> Colby **claps** loudly. (*How* does Colby clap? *loudly* Here ***claps*** is intransitive.)

CHAPTER 4

Identifying Direct and Indirect Objects, and Transitive and Intransitive Verbs

In each sentence, underline the verb or verb phrase. Above each boldfaced word write **DO, IO,** or **ADV** for direct object, indirect object, or adverb. On the line to the right, write whether the verb is **Transitive** or **Intransitive.**

1. Each of us told the **group** a **story.** ______________
2. Andrea narrated a **tale** of terror and bloodshed. ______________
3. Everyone was listening very **carefully.**
4. Who wrote **"The Pit and the Pendulum"**? ______________
5. Marcus gave **us** a **lesson** in pronunciation. ______________
6. Joe read the **class** a **poem.** ______________
7. Gordon was writing **Katrina** a long **letter.** ______________
8. Anna spoke **indistinctly.** ______________
9. Peter and Al presented a little **skit.** ______________
10. Peter played the **part** of a policeman. ______________

Name ______________________________ Date ______________

Lesson 2

Action Verbs and Objects

More Practice

A. Identifying Direct and Indirect Objects, and Transitive and Intransitive Verbs

In each sentence, underline the verb or verb phrase. Above each boldfaced word write **DO, IO,** or **ADV** for direct object, indirect object, or adverb. On the line at the right, write whether the verb is **Transitive** or **Intransitive.**

1. Louise started that **rumor.** ______________
2. She told several **classmates** a nasty **story** about her friends. ______________
3. She was lying **shamelessly.** ______________
4. Thomas repeated the **tale.** ______________
5. He told his **friends** a slightly different **version.** ______________
6. Friends of the victims reacted **angrily.** ______________
7. They told the **principal everything.** ______________
8. He has given **Louise and Thomas detention** for a week. ______________
9. Eloise never repeats **gossip.** ______________
10. She speaks **truthfully.** ______________

CHAPTER 4

B. Completing Transitive Verbs by Adding Direct Objects

Add a direct object to each of these sentences.

1. Public service announcements give listeners ______________ about various topics.
2. During blizzards, radio stations report ______________.
3. They must verify their ______________ before making their announcements.
4. Traffic announcers report ______________ on the roads.
5. Photographers shoot ______________ of unusual occurrences.
6. Sportscasters tell viewers______________ of the latest games.
7. Sometimes news bulletins interrupt ______________.
8. During tornado alerts, viewers get ______________ from local TV and radio stations.
9. A few hours after voting booths close, TV stations tell us ______________.
10. Yesterday I watched______________ on the TV.

Name ______________________ Date ____________

Lesson 2

Action Verbs and Objects

Application

A. Changing Intransitive Verbs to Transitive Verbs by Adding Direct Objects

The verb in each sentence below is an intransitive verb, without a direct object. Rewrite the sentence, using the same subject and verb but changing the rest of the sentence to make the verb transitive. Underline both the verb and the direct object that you add.

EXAMPLE The clown juggled skillfully.
The clown juggled six colored balls at one time.

1. Elena paints well.

____

2. Hans studied for an hour.

____

3. Olive practiced earlier today.

____

4. The boys will learn quickly.

____

5. The late-comers watched from the back of the auditorium.

____

CHAPTER 4

B. Using Direct and Indirect Objects and Transitive and Intransitive Verbs

Write a paragraph about hearing or telling a made-up story or presenting a factual report about true events. In the paragraph, use at least four terms from each box. Use the verbs as either transitive or intransitive verbs. Use the nouns and pronouns as direct or indirect objects. Underline each verb you use as a transitive verb.

Verbs			
told	reported	stated	called
spoke	learned	showed	helped
put	gave	taught	enjoyed

Nouns and Pronouns			
story	report	photo	girl
facts	event	news	boy
her	him	us	them

____

____

____

____

____

____

Name ______________________ Date ______________

Lesson 3

Linking Verbs and Predicate Words

Teaching

A linking verb connects the subject of a sentence to a word or words in the predicate. This word is called a **subject complement.** The subject complement identifies or describes the subject. Some common linking verbs are *is, feel, seem,* and *look.*

Costumes **are** clothing. (linking verb: *are;* subject complement: *clothing*)

Some costumes **look** fancy. (linking verb: look; subject complement: *fancy*)

There are two kinds of subject complements.

A **predicate noun** is a noun or pronoun that follows a linking verb and identifies, renames, or defines the subject.

Uniforms **are** my favorite costumes. (The predicate noun *costumes* identifies the subject, *uniforms.*)

A **predicate adjective** is an adjective that follows a linking verb and describes or modifies the subject.

That uniform **looks** really cool. (The predicate adjective *cool* describes the subject, *uniform.*)

Identifying Linking Verbs and Predicate Words

In each sentence, underline the subject once and the verb twice. Write the predicate word on the line to the right.

1. Flamenco is a traditional dance from southern Spain. ______
2. Brightly colored dresses are the costume of female flamenco dancers. ______
3. These beautiful dresses look frilly. ______
4. The skirts are ruffled. ______
5. Flowers are part of the women's costumes. ______
6. The dancers' jewelry looks colorful. ______
7. Their shoes sound noisy. ______
8. The men's bolero jackets seem short. ______
9. Do the jackets feel tight? ______
10. A key part of the costume is a black hat. ______
11. Flamenco dancers seem very energetic. ______
12. Are Spanish Gypsies the best flamenco dancers? ______

Name ____________________ Date ____________

Lesson 3 Linking Verbs and Predicate Words

More Practice

A. Identifying Linking Verbs and Predicate Words

In each sentence, underline the subject once and the verb twice. Write the predicate noun or predicate adjective on the line to the right.

1. A traditional Japanese garment is a kimono. ____________
2. A kimono is a robe like a wraparound for the body. ____________
3. Today, kimonos are clothing for special occasions only. ____________
4. An obi is a sash around a kimono. ____________
5. Zori are thong sandals. ____________
6. Pink kimonos seem popular with young girls. ____________
7. Black is the color of a formal kimono for married women. ____________
8. The silk kimono with the floral design seems expensive. ____________
9. This cotton kimono feels comfortable. ____________
10. The wedding kimono with the crane design looks beautiful. ____________

CHAPTER 4

B. Using Predicate Words

Complete each sentence by writing a predicate complement in the blank. In the parentheses following the sentence, write **PN** if you added a predicate noun or **PA** if you added a predicate adjective.

1. The brown cowboy boots with the pointy toes look ____________. (____)
2. My favorite shoes are my ____________. (____)
3. For us, the favorite costume day is ____________. (____)
4. At New Year's Eve, people are usually____________ about a new beginning. (____)
5. The clothing of party-goers seems particularly ____________. (____)
6. Their noise-makers sound especially ____________ at midnight. (____)
7. The uniforms of sports teams are, in a sense, a ____________. (____)
8. This bicycle helmet feels ____________. (____)
9. Those flippers worn by scuba divers are ____________. (____)
10. Snowshoes appear ____________, but they are effective. (____)

Name ______________________________ Date ______________

Lesson 3

Linking Verbs and Predicate Words

Application

A. Identifying Linking Verbs and Predicate Words

In each sentence, underline the subject once and the verb twice. Write the predicate word on the line to the right. After the predicate word, identify it by writing **PN** for predicate noun or **PA** for predicate adjective.

EXAMPLE Many knights of the king were soldiers in armor. *soldiers, PN*

1. For many centuries, the costume of a rich soldier was armor. ____________
2. Mail armor is rings of iron in a linked pattern. ____________
3. Suits of armor appear very uncomfortable. ____________
4. Plate armor from the 15th century is solid metal. ____________
5. A gauntlet is plate armor for a knight's hand and wrist. ____________
6. A suit of armor felt hot in the sun. ____________
7. The fasteners for a knight's armor were leather straps. ____________
8. Did walking knights sound creaky? ____________

CHAPTER 4

B. Using Linking Verbs and Predicate Words

Change the predicate word for each sentence in Exercise A. When possible, replace predicate nouns with predicate adjectives, and predicate adjectives with predicate nouns. Add other words in the predicate as needed.

EXAMPLE Many knights of the king were *loyal followers. OR*
Many knights of the king were *courageous.*

1. For many centuries, the costume of a rich soldier was ____________________
2. Mail armor is ____________________.
3. Suits of armor appear ____________________.
4. Plate armor from the 15th century is ____________________.
5. A gauntlet is ____________________.
6. A suit of armor felt ____________________.
7. The fasteners for a knight's armor were ____________________.
8. Did walking knights sound ____________________?

Name ______________________ Date ____________

Lesson 4

Principal Parts of Verbs

Teaching

Every verb has four basic forms called its **principal parts:** the present, the present participle, the past, and the past participle. With helping verbs, these four parts make all the tenses and forms of the verb.

I enjoy Mozart's music. (Present)
I am enjoying this performance. (Present participle)
I enjoyed past concerts. (Past)
I have enjoyed his works for years. (Past participle)

The Four Principal Parts of a Verb

Present	Present Participle	Past	Past Participle
enjoy	(is) enjoying	enjoyed	(has) enjoyed
listen	(is) listening	listened	(has) listened

There are two kinds of verbs: regular and irregular.

A **regular verb** is a verb whose past and past participle are formed by adding *–ed* or *–d* to the present. The present participle is formed by adding *–ing* to the present. Spelling changes are needed in some words, for example, *carr**y**-carr**ie**d.*

Regular Verbs

Present	Present Participle	Past	Past Participle
enjoy	(is) enjoy + **ing**	enjoy + **ed**	(has) enjoy + **ed**

Irregular verbs are discussed in the next lesson.

CHAPTER 4

Identifying Forms of Regular Verbs

Identify each underlined principal part of the verb. Write **Pres., Pres. Part., Past,** or **Past Part.** on the line to identify the present, present participle, past, or past participle form.

EXAMPLE The conductor has chosen the music for the concert. *Past Part.*

1. Wolfgang Amadeus Mozart composed more than 600 works. ____________
2. The orchestra has performed dozens of them. ____________
3. Tonight they are playing the *Haffner Symphony.* ____________
4. They often present his piano sonatas. ____________
5. His operas feature great characterizations. ____________
6. Mozart died at age 35. ____________
7. He was buried in a pauper's grave. ____________
8. It is not known who commissioned Mozart's *Requiem.* ____________
9. Some people have suggested that Mozart wrote it for himself. ____________
10. The college choral group is presenting the *Requiem* at tonight's concert. ____________

Name ______________________________ Date ______________

Lesson 4

Principal Parts of Verbs

More Practice

A. Identifying Forms of Regular Verbs

Identify each underlined principal part of the verb. Write **Pres., Pres. Part., Past,** or **Past Part.** to identify the present, present participle, past, or past participle form.

1. Rita's forgetting the book caused a delay. ______
2. The sleepy baby is making a fuss over his missing blanket. ______
3. When is the bus stopping here? ______
4. We are attempting to work the problem now. ______
5. Who in this room likes radishes? ______
6. Martha considered her schedule before making plans. ______
7. Henry played his heart out, but his team lost anyway. ______
8. We have wondered about the ending of that story. ______
9. I agree to your compromise. ______
10. They are forming a new governing board now. ______

CHAPTER 4

B. Writing the Correct Forms of Verbs

Decide which form of the verb given in parentheses is needed. Write the correct form on the line.

EXAMPLE Mozart had (compose) several sonatas by age 12. *composed*

1. Critics have (praise) Mozart for his taste and technique. ______
2. We particularly (respond) to his melodies. ______
3. Mozart was (compose) music when he was five. ______
4. He first (perform) in concert from about age seven. ______
5. I am (learn) to play a song from *The Marriage of Figaro* on the piano. ______
6. I have (like) that tune since the first time I heard it. ______
7. The first audiences (love) the comedy of *Figaro* as well as the music. ______
8. The local opera company is (present) the opera this weekend. ______
9. My cousin will be (play) the part of Cherubino. ______
10. Musicians ever since Mozart's time have (imitate) him. ______

Name ______________________ Date ______________

Lesson 4

Principal Parts of Verbs

Application

B. Writing the Correct Forms of Verbs

Decide which form of the verb given in parentheses is needed. Write the correct form on the line. Then identify which form you have used. Write **Pres., Pres. Part., Past,** or **Past Part.** to identify the present, present participle, past, or past participle form.

EXAMPLE The traffic has (stop) at the light. *stopped, Past Part.*

1. The police are (question) the suspect. ______________

2. The queen had (assign) the knights a difficult task. ______________

3. We (paint) the house last summer. ______________

4. The paint had (start) to peel. ______________

5. All summer, the painters (work) on it. ______________

6. Harriet was (clean) her room. ______________

7. I (clean) the garage every week. ______________

8. Mom (serve) tuna fish salad yesterday. ______________

9. The team has (play) twice this year and has lost both times. ______________

10. Who will be (face) us in the playoffs? ______________

CHAPTER 4

B. Supplying Verbs in the Correct Forms

Almost all the verbs other than helping verbs are missing from this paragraph. Choose the verb from the box that best completes each sentence. Be sure to use the correct verb form.

play	include	tap
die	compose	listen
travel	force	direct

Have you ever ______________ to *A Little Night Music* by Wolfgang Amadeus Mozart? It ______________ several lively melodies. The music is so cheerful that it ______________ you to hum or whistle along. If you can't carry a tune, you will be ______________ time to the music. The young man who ______________ the music was a musical prodigy. He ______________ violin and harpsichord almost as an infant, and was a composer by the age of five. As a child, he ______________ all over Europe with his father and sister, giving concerts. In his teens he was ______________ orchestras. Unfortunately, he ______________ young, at the age of 35.

Name ______________________ Date ______________

Lesson 5

Irregular Verbs

Reteaching

Irregular verbs are verbs whose past and past participle are not formed by adding *–ed* or *–d* to the present. The five sections of this chart show different patterns used to form the past and past participles of many irregular verbs.

	Present	Past	Past Participle
Group 1 The forms of the present, past, & past participle are same	burst cost hurt let put set shut	burst cost hurt let put set shut	(have) burst (have) cost (have) hurt (have) let (have) put (have) set (have) shut
Group 2 The forms of past & past participle are same	bring catch get lead sit	brought caught got led sat	(has) brought (has) caught (has) got (has) led (has) sat
Group 3 The past participle is formed by adding *-n* or *-en* to the past.	break choose freeze lie speak wear	broke chose froze lay spoke wore	(have) broken (have) chosen (have) frozen (have) lain (have) spoken (have) worn

	Present	Past	Past Participle
Group 4 The past participle is formed from the present, often adding *-n, -en,* or *-ne.*	do eat fall five go know run see take throw	did ate fell gave went knew ran saw took threw	(have) done (have) eaten (have) fallen (have) given (have) gone (have) known (have) run (have) seen (have) taken (have) thrown
Group 5 The last vowel changes from *i* in the present to *a* in the past, to *u* in the past participle.	begin drink ring sing sink swim	began drank rang sang sunk swam	(have) begun (have) drunk (have) rung (have) sung (have) sank (have) swum

The different forms of the verb *be* do not follow any pattern.

Present	Past	Past Participle
am, is, are	was, were	(have) been

Using the Correct Forms of Irregular Verbs

Underline the correct verb form of the two in parentheses.

1. The judges have (chose, chosen) the finalists.
2. Our mayor has not (broke, broken) any promises.
3. Everyone (drank, drunk) milk with the sandwiches.
4. Soccer fans (began, begun) to fill the stands an hour before the game.
5. Have you (brung, brought) your application with you?
6. We (did, done) an experiment showing the effects of global warming.
7. Rabbits (ate, eaten) most of the lettuce in our garden.
8. I haven't (gave, given) my poetry reading yet.
9. My summer vacation certainly (went, gone) quickly.
10. Very few people (knew, known) about the secret room.
11. Grapes have (grew, grown) in this valley for years.
12. The last of the marathon entrants has (run, ran) past the finish line.

CHAPTER 4

Name ________________________________ Date ________________

Lesson 5

Irregular Verbs

More Practice

A. Using the Correct Forms of Irregular Verbs

Underline the correct verb form of the two in parentheses.

1. The barbershop quartet (sang, sung) in close harmony.
2. I (saw, seen) a hilarious sitcom on television last night.
3. My teacher must have (spoke, spoken) to the coach.
4. The soprano (took, taken) an extra breath for her high notes.
5. The seal (swam, swum) to the rocky island.
6. Two players were (threw, thrown) out of the game.
7. A burgler has (stole, stolen) the diamond jewelry.
8. Jane (wrote, written) several papers on the computer last week.
9. The milk must have (froze, frozen) on the porch.
10. A baby robin has (fell, fallen) out of the nest.
11. The principal (rang, rung) the fire alarm.
12. We have (shook, shaken) the tree to get some apples to fall.

B. Writing the Correct Forms of Verbs

Decide which form is needed: the present participle, the past, or the past participle of each verb given in parentheses. Write the correct form on the line.

EXAMPLE The squirrels have (steal) the birdfeed. *stolen*

1. Amiko (choose) her library books yesterday. ____________
2. My favorite jeans have (begin) to wear out. ____________
3. Someone (break) that valuable Chinese vase. ____________
4. Why didn't you (bring) your skateboard? ____________
5. The cattle have (eat) the corn and oats. ____________
6. Patty has (do) twice as much research as Ron. ____________
7. No, I have never (drink) coconut milk. ____________
8. Another spacecraft (go) into orbit around the moon. ____________
9. My father has (give) me a new pair of skates. ____________
10. My hair (grow) two inches during the vacation. ____________

Name ______________________ Date ______________

Lesson 5

Irregular Verbs

Application

A. Writing the Correct Forms of Verbs

Decide which form of the verb given in parentheses is needed. Write the correct form on the line. Identify the form you used by writing **Present, Past,** or **PP** for *past participle.*

EXAMPLE The horse (spring) into action at Roy's call. *sprang, Past*

1. Currently, the police (know) of no motive for the crime. ______________
2. Have you (speak) to anyone about your vacation plans? ______________
3. Who (see) your solar calculator last? ______________
4. The senior choir has (sing) a medley of show tunes. ______________
5. Our lawn mower (run) out of gas before I finished the lawn. ______________
6. Who could have (steal) such a heavy statue? ______________
7. I have (write) several poems for the school newspaper. ______________
8. The team (swim) warm-up laps before the meet. ______________
9. Who has (take) the schedule off the bulletin board? ______________
10. The skittish pony (throw) everyone who tries to ride it. ______________

B. Proofreading for the Correct Forms of Verbs

Draw a line through each incorrect verb form in this paragraph. Draw this proofreading symbol ^ next to the error and, in the spaces between lines of type, write the correct form of the verb.

EXAMPLE In the past, Dad has ~~went~~ ^*gone* ice fishing with my uncle.

Last weekend I went ice-fishing for the first time with my dad and nearly freezed to death. I weared two pairs of wool socks, but needed about four. For six hours, we sitted in this little hut and fished through a hole in the ice, but the fish weren't biting. After a while, I begun to get hungry. When I told my dad, he opened a can of cold sardines, and we eat them with some stale crackers.

CHAPTER 4

Name ______________________________ Date ______________

Lesson 6

Simple Tenses

Teaching

A **tense** is a verb form that shows the time of an action or condition. Verbs have three **simple tenses:** the present, the past, and the future. The **present tense** shows an action or condition that occurs now. The **past tense** shows an action or condition that was completed in the past. The **future tense** shows an action or condition that will occur in the future.

Present	Rain **aids** plant growth. Rain **is** helpful.
Past	Rain **aided** plant growth. Rain **was** helpful.
Future	Rain **will aid** plant growth. Rain **will be** helpful.

The progressive form of a verb shows an action or condition that is in progress. The progressive forms of the three simple tenses are used to show that actions are, were, or will be in progress.

Present Progressive	Rain **is aiding** plant growth.
Past Progressive	Rain **was aiding** plant growth.
Future Progressive	Rain **will be aiding** plant growth.

The **present tense** is the present principal part of the verb. The **past tense** is the past principal part. To form the **future tense,** add *will* to the present principal part.

Tense	Singular	Plural
Present	I aid / you aid / he, she, it aids	we aid / you aid / they aid
Past	I aided / you aided / he, she, it aided	we aided / you aided / they aided
Future	I will aid / you will aid / he, she, it will aid	we will aid / you will aid / they will aid

Form the present, past, and future progressive by using the forms of the verb *be* with the present participle of the verb, as in *I am talking, I was talking,* and *I will be talking.*

CHAPTER 4

Recognizing the Simple Tenses

Identify the tense of each underlined verb. On the line, label the tense: **Present, Past, Future,** or **Present P, Past P.,** or **Future P**. for *present, past,* or *future progressive.*

1. The sun is chasing the clouds away. ____________
2. It rained yesterday. ____________
3. It will be snowing before long. ____________
4. Clouds were darkening the sky to the west. ____________
5. The sun warms the earth. ____________
6. The warm night air will dry the puddles. ____________
7. The rain is spoiling our picnic plan. ____________
8. Rain promises future growth. ____________
9. Three months ago, snow was falling every day. ____________
10. In the morning, I will be rising early for our hike. ____________

Name ______________________________ Date ______________

Lesson 6

Simple Tenses

More Practice

A. Recognizing the Simple Tenses

Identify the tense of each underlined verb. On the line, label the tense: **Present, Past, Future,** or **Present P, Past P.,** or **Future P.** for *present, past,* or *future progressive.*

1. Are you planning a picnic? ______________
2. We will be organizing a baseball game. ______________
3. If it rains, we won't be able to play baseball. ______________
4. It rained last year, and we played baseball anyway. ______________
5. If it's windy, we will be flying kites. ______________
6. Last year I was paddling a canoe when it started raining. ______________
7. I paddled back to the boathouse in a hurry. ______________
8. We will barbecue again, won't we? ______________
9. I was hoping for a balloon-toss contest with water-filled balloons. ______________
10. I am looking forward to the event already. ______________

CHAPTER 4

B. Using the Simple Tenses

In each item, provide the form of the verb requested in parentheses.

1. (*predict,* present progressive) The meteorologists ______________ gradual cooling.
2. (*snow,* future) I'm sure it ______________ well before Christmas.
3. (*skate,* future progressive) We ______________ on the park lake before long.
4. (*sled,* past) Last year we ______________ in the park until the end of March.
5. (*skate,* present) Helen ______________ but prefers skiing.
6. (*play,* past) Ali ______________ hockey when she was younger.
7. (*play,* past progressive) She ______________ goalie when she got a broken arm.
8. (*wait,* present progressive) My dogs ______________ to go on a walk.
9. (*travel,* future progressive) Soon Eddie ______________ to Florida for a vacation.
10. (*enjoy,* past progressive) People there ______________ sunshine while we had snow storms.

Name ______________________________ Date ______________

Lesson 6

Simple Tenses

Application

A. Correcting Simple Tenses of Verbs

Although the times referred to in this paragraph vary from past to future, all of its verbs are in the present tense. Rewrite the paragraph, correcting verb tenses as needed. Use progressive tenses if the action is, was, or will be in progress. Underline every verb.

Today the sun shines brightly. Until the end of the week we enjoy warm weather. This contrasts with the weather last year. Last year at this time snow covers the ground. Ice causes trouble for vehicles and pedestrians. Personally, I prefer the unseasonably warm weather. I hope that next year the warm temperatures return.

____

____

____

____

____

____

CHAPTER 4

B. Using Verb Forms Correctly

For each verb on the list, write the form requested in parentheses. Then write a paragraph about a topic of your choice that uses at least four of the phrases. Make sure all verb forms are used correctly.

(*find,* present) I ______________

(*listen,* past) I ______________

(*watch,* present progressive) I ______________

(*measure,* future) I ______________

(*compare,* future progressive) I ______________

(*observe,* past progressive) I ______________

____

____

____

____

____

____

____

Name ______________________________ Date ______________

Lesson 7

Perfect Tenses

Teaching

The **present perfect tense** shows an action or condition that began in the past and continues into the present.

Present Perfect Dan **has called** every day this week.

The past perfect tense shows an action or condition in the past that came before another action or condition in the past.

Past Perfect Dan **had called** before Ellen arrived.

The future perfect tense shows an action or condition in the future that will occur before another action or condition in the future.

Future Perfect Dan **will have called** before Ellen arrives.

To form the **present perfect, past perfect,** and **future perfect tenses,** add *has, have, had,* or *will have* to the past participle.

Tense	Singular	Plural
Present Perfect has or have + past participle	I have called you have called he, she, it has called	we have called you have called they have called
Past Perfect had + past participle	I had called you had called he, she, it had called	we had called you had called they had called
Future Perfect will + have + past participle	I will have called you will have called he, she, it will have called	we will have called you will have called they will have called

CHAPTER 4

Recognizing the Perfect Tenses

Underline the verb in each sentence. On the blank, write the tense of the verb.

1. The film house has not developed the pictures yet. ______________

2. Fred will have left before Erin's arrival. ______________

3. Florence has been a vary gracious hostess. ______________

4. Andi had lost her transfer by the end of the bus ride. ______________

5. By tonight, I will have finished my assignment. ______________

6. Before the discovery of the buried chest, Joe had not believed in buried treasure. ______________

7. We have worked over an hour on one math problem. ______________

8. Until his college years, Carl had not decided on his career. ______________

9. The snow plows had cleared our street before the really heavy snowstorm. ______________

10. Have the Ortons found their dog yet? ______________

Name ______________________ Date ______________

Lesson 7

Perfect Tenses

More Practice

A. Recognizing the Perfect Tenses

Underline the verb in each sentence. On the blank, write the tense of the verb.

1. Olga had figured out the answer before her teacher's explanation. ______________
2. I have walked every day now for a month. ______________
3. Vickie had liked Nels until their argument. ______________
4. Alf will have jogged 70 miles by the end of next week. ______________
5. By lunch time, Rusty had started cooking dinner. ______________
6. Ira has practiced piano every day for a week. ______________
7. At this rate, we will not have finished the 30 chapters by June. ______________
8. Our HMO has added a number of new physicians to the staff. ______________
9. The ice on the lake will have melted long before the weekend. ______________
10. The window had cracked before the wind storm. ______________

CHAPTER 4

B. Forming the Perfect Tenses

Complete each sentence by writing the form of the verb indicated in parentheses.

1. (*finish*, past perfect) We ______________ our game before the Meteors started theirs.
2. (*graduate*, future perfect) Margie ______________ before the spring semester.
3. (*vote*, past perfect) Union members ______________ before they saw the contract.
4. (*exercise*, present perfect) We ______________ three times this week.
5. (*talk*, past perfect) The manager ______________ to the pitcher twice by that time.
6. (*clean*, future perfect) I ______________ the whole kitchen by the time Mom returns.
7. (*offer*, present perfect) Angelica frequently ______________ to help.
8. (*produce*, future perfect) By the end of this writing course, you ______________ a plot outline and at least four chapters of your novel.
9. (*picked*, past perfect) He ______________ ten bushels before the truck showed up.
10. (*search*, present perfect) The rescuers ______________ the area for hours.

Name ____________________ Date ____________

Lesson 7

Perfect Tenses

Application

A. Using Verb Tenses

The following is a journal entry of a girl of the mid-1800s in a wagon train heading for California. Supply verbs to the narrative in the tenses indicated in parentheses. Use verbs from the list below.

be, expect, walk, insist, pack, lose

The first month on the trail (present perfect) ____________ challenging. Before we set out, I (past perfect) ____________ that I would ride the wagon, but instead I (present perfect) ____________ miles every day. Mother (present perfect) ____________ that I always wear a bonnet because of the sun. It's a good thing that we (past perfect) ____________ so many bonnets, because the wind keeps blowing them off my head and across the prairie! I think I (future perfect) ____________ all my bonnets before we arrive in California.

B. Using Verb Tenses

Choose a trip you have made or would like to make. Write sentences about the trip using the following verbs in the tenses indicated.

1. see (future) ____________

2. pack (present perfect) ____________

3. hope (past progressive) ____________

4. visit (future perfect) ____________

5. be (past perfect) ____________

6. learn (past progressive) ____________

7. try (future perfect) ____________

Name ______________________________ Date ______________

Lesson 8 Using Verb Tenses

Teaching

In writing and speaking, you use the tenses of verbs to indicate when events happen. Changing tenses indicates a change in time. If you do not need to indicate a change in time between two actions, keep the tenses of verbs the same.

The Present Tenses These tenses show events occurring in the present time:

Present	Action occurs in the present.	count, counts
Present perfect	Action began in past and continues in present.	has counted, have counted
Present progressive	Action is in progress now.	is counting, are counting

The Past Tenses These tenses show events occurring in a past time:

Past	Action began and ended in the past.	counted
Past perfect	Action began and ended before another event in the past.	had counted
Past progressive	Action in the past was ongoing.	was counting

The Future Tenses These tenses show events occurring in a future time:

Future	Action will occur in the future.	will count
Future perfect	Action will occur in the future before another action in the future.	will have counted
Future progressive	Action in the future will be ongoing.	will be counting

CHAPTER 4

Using Verb Tenses

Underline the verb form in parentheses that correctly completes each sentence.

1. In normal activities, we usually (use, had used) ten as our base for counting.

2. Last night, whoever (counted, will count) sheep did so on a base ten system.

3. Tomorrow, children (have used, will use) their fingers to find answers to math facts.

4. Long ago, our counting system (developed, develops) with the base of ten.

5. Obviously, using ten (came, will be coming) easily because of our ten fingers.

6. Some of the oldest writings still in existence (had shown, show) counting by ten.

7. Over 2,000 years ago, Romans (were using, will be using) ten-based numerals.

8. Since the founding of the country, the U.S. government (has produced, will produce) coins and bills based on a decimal system.

9. Yet a ten-based system is not the only one you (have used, had used) today.

10. A clock (has counted, counts) to twelve and then starts over.

11. Before an hour passed, sixty minutes (had passed, are passing).

12. A week (consisted, consists) of seven days, not ten.

Name ______________________ Date ______________

Lesson 8

Using Verb Tenses

More Practice

A. Using Verb Tenses

Underline the verb form in parentheses that correctly completes each sentence.

1. For thousands of years, people (have recognized, are recognizing) the need for standard measurements.

2. What would happen if different construction crews at the same site (were using, will use) rulers of different lengths?

3. For many centuries, such problems (were occurring, are occurring) frequently.

4. Today, we (were avoiding, avoid) problems by using standardized measurements.

5. In the past, each carpenter (measured, measures) a foot according to his own foot.

6. Over time, each country (set, will be setting) standards of weights and measures.

7. At last, many scientists (will agree, agreed) on a common set of standards.

8. The metric system (had related, relates) measures of length, weight, heat, force, and other quantities.

9. By 1950, almost all countries (had adopted, are adopting) the metric system.

10. In the future, even the United States (has adopted, will adopt) the metric system.

B. Correcting Sentence Order

The sentences of this story are out of order. Read the story. Use the verb tenses and context to determine the correct order. Then rewrite the story in paragraph form below, with the sentences in correct order.

Before my parents took their first cruise, my family had traveled together.
All of us will see glaciers and the midnight sun.
Now they are planning a cruise for the whole family.
They really enjoyed the cruise.
This time they want to go to Alaska.
For example, we had traveled to the Grand Canyon.
Then my parents took a cruise to the Caribbean.

____

____

____

____

____

____

____

CHAPTER 4

Name ______________________________ Date ______________

Lesson 8

Using Verb Tenses

Application

A. Correcting Verb Tenses

Each underlined verb is in an incorrect tense. Write a correct form of the verb on the line.

1. Next June, my parents have been married for fifteen years. ______________
2. After the old tapestry had been cleaned, the museum staff hangs it carefully. ______________
3. When the sun came out, the children's snowman will melt. ______________
4. A penny had been worth one-tenth of a dime and one-hundredth of a dollar. ______________
5. For this past week, the train will be arriving on time. ______________
6. When we lost our electric power, we are watching my favorite sitcom. ______________
7. Before Maizie won a race, she is competing in several races unsuccessfully. ______________
8. Danita kept forgetting her lines while she is acting in the play. ______________
9. I had checked the price of this coat in several stores before I am buying it. ______________
10. While Dave mows the lawn, his sister washed the windows. ______________

CHAPTER 4

B. Correcting Sentence Order

Some of the verbs in this paragraph are in the wrong tense. Decide which verbs must be changed. Write the numbers of these sentences below. Then rewrite those sentences, correcting those verbs. Underline the verbs you have changed.

(1) For my grandparents' 50th wedding anniversary, my parents, aunts, and uncles bought them tickets for a cruise. **(2)** They said it was a small payback for all my grandparents are doing for them through the years. **(3)** And it's something they remember for the rest of their lives. **(4)** By the time my grandparents return, they will have been gone almost three weeks. **(5)** By then they will visit Barbados, St. Thomas, and other islands. **(6)** I hope they were enjoying the cruise now. **(7)** With luck, they have a great time.

____

____

____

____

____

Name ______________________________ Date ____________

Lesson 9 Troublesome Verb Pairs

Teaching

Do not confuse these pairs of verbs. Read how they differ, and study the chart.

lie/lay *Lie* means "to rest or recline." It does not take an object.
Lay means "to put or place something." It does take an object.

set/sit *Sit* means "to be in a seat" or "to rest." It does not take an object.
Set means "to put or place something." It does take an object.

rise/raise *Rise* means "to move upward" or "to get up." It does not take an object.
Raise means "to lift (something) up." It usually takes an object.

leave/let *Leave* means "to depart" or "to allow something to remain where it is."
Let means "to allow" or "permit." Both *leave* and *let* may take objects.

	Present	Past	Past Participle
Lie / Lay	**lie** My sister lies in a crib.	**lay** I lay down for a nap.	**lain** Others have lain there.
	lay Al lays a book here.	**laid** He laid a book there.	**laid** He has laid two books down.
Sit / Set	**sit** Jeff sits there.	**sat** Jeff sat there before.	**sat** Jeff has sat there often.
	set Ann sets her hair.	**set** Ann set it last night.	**set** She has set it nightly.
Rise / Raise	**rise** We rise at 8 A.M.	**rose** We rose early.	**risen** You have risen early.
	raise Fay raises the flag.	**raised** I raised it before.	**raised** Fay has raised it.
Leave / Let	**leave** Leave the bike here.	**left** You left your dog here.	**left** You have left a cat too.
	let Let me ride your bike.	**let** I let the dog come in.	**let** I have let the cat go out.

CHAPTER 4

Using Troublesome Verbs Correctly

Underline the correct verb in parentheses.

1. That school (lets, leaves) both boys and girls try out for the baseball team.
2. Don't (let, leave) your camera in a hot place for too long.
3. You had better (let, leave) the traffic clear before you try to cross this highway.
4. No one may (sit, set) in the bleachers during band practice.
5. We usually (sit, set) on the porch steps and talk about the news of the day.
6. The cat (lay, laid) in front of the fire all afternoon.
7. I think you have (laid, lain) in the sun too long.
8. I (rose, raised) at 5:00 this morning because I couldn't sleep.
9. The ship's owners hope to be able to (rise, raise) the sunken ship.
10. (Let, Leave) the lasagna bake in the oven for forty-five minutes.
11. To avoid accidents, (sit, set) that vase in the center of the table.
12. Who (lay, laid) this rake on the ground with its tines up?

Name ______________________________ Date ______________

Lesson 9

Troublesome Verb Pairs

More Practice

A. Using Troublesome Verbs Correctly

Underline the correct verb in parentheses.

1. Meg (sat, set) her science project on the teacher's desk.
2. Someone (let, left) the car windows open.
3. The dog is (setting, sitting) under the tree enjoying the shade.
4. The patient must (lie, lay) perfectly still during the X-ray.
5. The family won't (let, leave) the occasion pass without a celebration.
6. The divers had (raised, risen) to the surface.
7. The platypus at the zoo (lay, laid) an egg yesterday.
8. The curtain (rose, raised) on the last act of the class play.
9. We (let, left) our car at the airport when we flew to visit our grandparents.
10. Sam (set, sit) the mysterious brown package on the table.

B. Correcting Troublesome Verbs

Examine the boldfaced verb in each of the following sentences. If the verb is not correct, write the proper verb on the line. If the verb is correct, write **Correct.**

CHAPTER 4

1. We **laid** our towels on the beach before running into the water. ______________
2. Will the police **leave** us go through the barricade? ______________
3. If you do not **raise** an objection, the motion may pass. ______________
4. Help me **lie** these ceramic tiles in place. ______________
5. Sometimes it's hard for babies to **set** long enough to have their picture taken. ______________
6. Tomorrow, I shall **lay** in the sun and relax. ______________
7. The bread should **raise** if the yeast is good. ______________
8. **Set** aside any doubts you may have. ______________
9. Steve has **left** his car run out of gas. ______________
10. The tools were **lying** in that metal box. ______________
11. Did your sister **sit** the cover over the cake after she took some? ______________
12. Larry fell asleep two minutes after he had **laid** down. ______________

Name ______________________________ Date ______________

Lesson 9

Troublesome Verb Pairs

Application

A. Correcting Troublesome Verbs

Examine the boldfaced verb in each of the following sentences. If the verb is not correct, write the proper verb on the line. If the verb is correct, write **Correct.**

1. Throughout the game, we had to **set** in the bleachers. ______________
2. Before the parade started, Rose and George **rose** the banner. ______________
3. The guards waited for the shoplifter to **leave** the store. ______________
4. Why don't you **lay** down until your headache goes away. ______________
5. The newspaper **set** on the doorstep waiting to be picked up. ______________
6. This new race car will **leave** the rest of them in the dust. ______________
7. The firemen **set** the old house on fire as a training exercise for their new firefighters. ______________
8. You'd better not **leave** your dog out of your sight. ______________
9. John is working very hard to **raise** enough money to buy a new TV. ______________
10. Thea **lay** out all the things to pack before putting them in the suitcase. ______________

CHAPTER 4

B. Using Troublesome Verbs Correctly

The following sentences contain five incorrectly used verbs. Rewrite the paragraph below, correcting all five errors.

Every year, right about this time, the same idea raises in my mind. The idea is that I'm working too hard. I sit here thinking that I need a vacation. Let the rest of the world raise at the crack of dawn. I need to lay in bed another hour or two or three. I need to just set and read all day. "Leave me alone," I want to tell the whole world. "Leave me rest."

____

____

____

____

____

____

____

____

Name ______________________ Date ____________

Lesson 1 What Is an Adjective?

Teaching

An **adjective** is a word that modifies, or describes, a noun or a pronoun. Adjectives answer the questions *what kind, which one, how many,* or *how much.*

Adjectives	
What kind?	steep trail, green meadow
Which one or ones?	first stream
How many or how much?	four hikers, much food

Articles

The most commonly used adjectives are the articles *a, an* and *the. A* and *an* are **indefinite articles.** They refer to someone or something in general. Use *a* before a word beginning with a consonant or a long "u" sound and *an* before a word beginning with a vowel.

We took a hike in the mountains. A uniformed ranger led us. It was an adventure!

The is the **definite article**. It points out a specific person, place, thing, or idea.

Do you have the map?

Proper Adjectives

Many adjectives are formed from common nouns, such as *sandy* from *sand.* **Proper adjectives** are formed from a proper noun. Proper adjectives are always capitalized.

Proper Noun	Proper Adjective
Asia	Asian
Mexico	Mexican

CHAPTER 5

Identifying Adjectives

Underline all the adjectives in each sentence, including the articles.

1. A friend and I recently took a trip to the Swiss Alps.
2. We saw beautiful scenery and got great exercise.
3. We carried heavy backpacks with everything we needed.
4. Leigha brought a nylon tent, while I had the food.
5. We hiked several miles each day, usually to the farthest campsite we could reach.
6. We had a good time visiting the oldtime villages along the way.
7. Sometimes we hiked all day to reach the nearest village.
8. We had a wonderful trip with no bad accidents.
9. The biggest challenge we faced was a deep river that we couldn't cross.
10. Once, a case of bad map-reading made us walk five extra miles.
11. When we reached one village, we treated ourselves to a delicious meal.
12. For dessert, we ordered a rich chocolate torte.
13. We loved the peace of the ancient mountains.
14. We will remember the amazing hike for many years.

Name ______________________________ Date ______________

Lesson 1

What Is an Adjective?

More Practice

A. Identifying Adjectives and the Words They Modify

Underline each adjective once and the word it modifies twice. Circle the proper adjectives. Ignore the articles.

1. Two old prospectors and a weary mule trudged across the desert.
2. The loyal fans cheered the team in the final game.
3. The lunch consisted of homemade soup and English muffins.
4. The European guests told interesting stories of the trip.
5. Several silly clowns wore baggy pants.
6. Many American tourists visit sunny Mexican beaches.
7. Antique jewelry got top prices at the auction.
8. A few fine museums in major cities exhibit Greek statues.
9. Floral wallpaper was put up in the front hall.
10. The chef put Italian sausage into the hearty stew.

B. Writing Adjectives

Write an adjective to complete each sentence.

Example *My class hiked up a small mountain before we graduated.*

1. At the base there were two paths, and we took the ______________ one.
2. We wanted to take a ______________ path to the mountain top.
3. There were ______________ tree roots and loose rocks along the way.
4. It was pretty easy, though, until we reached a ______________ climb.
5. Some of my classmates started to wish we had taken an ______________ path instead.
6. We got to see some ______________ wildlife, such as squirrels, raccoons, and snakes.
7. At the top, we could probably see for at least ______________ miles.
8. The rest on the mountain top gave us a chance to have a ______________ lunch.
9. We noticed a ______________ raindrops and decided to start heading down.
10. Our ______________ foreign exchange student enjoyed spending time with us before she went back to her homeland.

CHAPTE

Name ______________________ Date ______________

Lesson 1

What Is an Adjective?

Application

A. Writing Adjectives in Sentences

Use the word at the beginning of each item as an adjective in a sentence.

Example scary *The camp counselor told a scary story.*

1. shiny ______________________
2. turquoise ______________________
3. rare ______________________
4. Asian ______________________
5. innocent ______________________
6. rainy ______________________
7. playful ______________________
8. easy ______________________
9. curious ______________________
10. Japanese ______________________

B. Writing a Paragraph Using Adjectives

Imagine that you are on an overnight hike in the mountains. How could you describe the scenery you see? What words could describe the people who have come with you on the hike? Write a short paragraph about an overnight hike. Use at least five adjectives in your description. Underline the adjectives in your paragraph.

Name ______________________________ Date ______________

Lesson 2

Predicate Adjectives

Teaching

A **predicate adjective** is an adjective that follows a linking verb and describes the verb's subject. The linking verb connects the predicate adjective with the subject.

> The sinking of the *Titanic* was totally disastrous. (The linking verbs is *was.* The predicate adjective is *disastrous.*)

Often, forms of *be* are linking verbs, as in the above example. However, predicate adjectives can also follow other linking verbs such as *taste, smell, feel, look, become,* and *seem.*

> Such a catastrophe seemed completely impossible. (The linking verbs is *seemed.* The predicate adjective is *impossible.*)

Identifying Predicate Adjectives

Underline the predicate adjective in each sentence. If the sentence has no predicate adjective, write **None** on the line to the right.

1. In 1912, of all the ships in the world, the *Titanic* was the largest. ______
2. Everyone thought it was unsinkable. ______
3. As the ship set out on its first voyage, the passengers felt jubilant. ______
4. However, the icebergs around the ship looked ominous. ______
5. As soon as the ship hit an iceberg, its sinking was inevitable. ______
6. The crew started loading women and children onto the lifeboats. ______
7. The number of lifeboats was not enough to carry all those aboard. ______
8. The passengers felt terrified. ______
9. The wireless radio operators kept sending distress signals. ______
10. Their efforts were useless. ______
11. The fate of the ship became obvious. ______
12. The sinking of the *Titanic* was rapid. ______
13. After the *Titanic* disaster, changes in the shipping industry were many. ______
14. Radio operations on ships must be always open. ______
15. The number of lifeboats must be adequate for passengers and crew. ______
16. Today, ship passengers can be certain of a safe voyage. ______

Name ____________________ Date ____________

Lesson 2

Predicate Adjectives

More Practice

A. Identifying Predicate Adjectives and the Words They Modify

Underline the predicate adjective in each of the following sentences. Write the word it modifies on the line to the right.

1. The huge crowd appeared excited. ____________
2. Our guests were weary after their long trip. ____________
3. Frank looked ridiculous in his baggy costume. ____________
4. The old gray mansion was famous for antique furniture. ____________
5. These old stamps might be valuable in the future. ____________
6. The floral wallpaper looks perfect in the hall. ____________
7. That chair is amazingly heavy for its size. ____________
8. In May, the lake is still too cold for swimming. ____________
9. Doesn't the kitten's fur feel soft? ____________
10. Something in the refrigerator smells rotten. ____________

B. Writing Predicate Adjectives

Complete each sentence with a predicate adjective. Write the predicate adjective on the line.

1. The *Titanic* was ____________.
2. At the beginning of the voyage, the passengers felt ____________.
3. The iceberg must have been ____________.
4. The lifeboats were ____________.
5. The crew seemed ____________.
6. The water, dotted with icebergs, must have been ____________.
7. It was ____________ to watch the *Titanic* sink.
8. After the disaster, everyone felt ____________.
9. Ship captains probably became more ____________ about traveling near icebergs.
10. Now, ships are ____________ than ever before.

CHAPTER 5

Name ______________________ Date ______________

Lesson 2

Predicate Adjectives

Application

A. Writing Predicate Adjectives in Sentences

Use the word at the beginning of each item as a predicate adjective in a sentence.

Example creative *Artists are creative.*

1. nervous ______________________

2. proud ______________________

3. young ______________________

4. truthful ______________________

5. joyful ______________________

6. wise ______________________

7. terrible ______________________

8. full ______________________

9. frightening ______________________

10. impossible ______________________

B. Writing a Paragraph Using Predicate Adjectives

A disaster such as the sinking of the *Titanic* brings out the best and the worst in people. Imagine that you are a survivor of the *Titanic*. Write a paragraph in which you recall how you felt on that night. Describe how the people around you acted and what happened to them and the ship. Use at least five predicate adjectives in your description. Use a verb other than a form of *be* in at least two of the sentences. Underline the predicate adjectives in your paragraph.

CHAPTER 5

Name ______________________________ Date ______________

Lesson 3

Other Words Used as Adjectives

Teaching

Some nouns and pronouns can be used as adjectives. They can modify nouns to make their meanings more specific.

Pronouns as Adjectives

This, that, these, and *those* are **demonstrative pronouns** that can be used as adjectives. *My, our, your, his, her, its,* and *their* are **possessive pronouns** that can be used as adjectives. **Indefinite pronouns** such as *all, each, both, few, many, most,* and *some* can be used as adjectives.

Demonstrative pronoun	That city was destroyed by a volcano.
Possessive pronoun	People died in their homes.
Indefinite pronoun	Many people were buried in the ashes.

Nouns as Adjectives Some nouns can be used as adjectives.

Noun	Pompeii lay beneath ash piles.

Identifying Nouns and Pronouns Used as Adjectives

Underline the nouns or pronouns that are used as adjectives in each sentence.

1. Pompeii was a thriving port town in ancient Italy.
2. Many wealthy Romans made their homes there.
3. On August 24, A.D. 79, the people of Pompeii started their morning routines.
4. That day would be different from all other days.
5. On that day, a volcano, Mount Vesuvius, erupted.
6. Lava streams poured out of this volcano.
7. Many people were buried in their homes.
8. Ash showers sprayed down on these unfortunate people.
9. The Pompeii disaster survived in legend, thanks to a writer named Pliny the Younger and his account of that day.
10. This man told in a letter how he led his mother to safety.
11. He wrote about his uncle who had died trying to save his friends.
12. That city was totally buried, and for many years no one could find its location.
13. In 1748, a peasant was digging in his vineyard and struck a stone wall.
14. Later, diggers uncovered more of the city of Pompeii, with its colorful wall paintings, artistic floor mosaics, and beautiful wine bottles.
15. Pompeii has become famous because its ruins are so well preserved.

CHAPTER 5

Name ______________________________ Date ______________

Lesson 3

Other Words Used as Adjectives

More Practice

A. Identifying Adjectives and the Words They Modify

Underline the pronouns or nouns used as adjectives in the following sentences. Draw an arrow from the adjective to the word it modifies.

1. Check your facts in this history book.
2. My parents bought those plants for their rock garden.
3. Each student filled out these forms on the first school day.
4. These ice cream toppings are delicious.
5. Some band members are competing in the music contest.
6. I decided to stay home after reading that movie review.
7. We finished our hike under the hot, afternoon sun.
8. The desert tortoise makes its home in the American Southwest.
9. Both players received their trophies at the awards dinner.
10. Most days, we can see Greg wearing his favorite flannel shirt and old denim jeans.

B. Using Pronouns as Adjectives

Complete each sentence with a pronoun that is used as an adjective. Write the word on the line.

1. People in ancient Pompeii ran from ______________ houses when the volcano erupted.
2. ______________ people tried to escape.
3. ______________ day must have been terrifying.
4. ______________ people remembered the story of Pompeii, and many stories were written about the calamity.
5. Centuries later, a peasant discovered Pompeii and ______________ treasures.
6. ______________ person who sees Pompeii is impressed by how well preserved it is.
7. ______________ artistic and architectural treasures amaze everyone.
8. The ______________ artworks still visible on the walls are beautiful.
9. If you travel to Italy, you should include a trip to Pompeii in ______________ plans.

CHAPTER 5

Name ______________________ Date ____________

Lesson 3 Other Words Used as Adjectives

Application

A. Writing Adjectives in Sentences

Use the word at the beginning of each item as an adjective in a sentence.

EXAMPLE tin *The rain was loud on the tin roof of the shed.*

1. my ______________________

2. wood ______________________

3. movie ______________________

4. music ______________________

5. each ______________________

6. some ______________________

7. many ______________________

8. your ______________________

9. these ______________________

10. television ______________________

B. Writing a Paragraph Using Pronouns and Nouns as Adjectives

Use five of the following nouns and pronouns as adjectives in a paragraph that describes a busy modern city. Write your paragraph on the lines below. Underline the words you use from the list.

city	office	your	every	that
street	car	their	many	those

____

____

____

____

____

____

____

____

____

CHAPTER 5

Name ______________________________ Date ____________

Lesson 4 What Is an Adverb?

Teaching

An **adverb** is a word that modifies a verb, an adjective, or another adverb. Adverbs answer the questions *how, when, where,* or *to what extent.*

Modifying a verb	Ernie never travels without an alarm clock.
Modifying an adjective	He is always careful about his luggage.
Modifying an adverb	He gets to the airport very early.

Intensifiers are adverbs that modify adjectives or other adverbs. They usually come directly before the word they modify. Intensifiers usually answer the question *To what extent?*

Adverbs	
How?	immediately, correctly
When?	soon, later
Where?	away, around
To what extent?	completely, entirely

Many adverbs are formed by adding the suffix *-ly* to adjectives. Sometimes a base word's spelling changes when *-ly* is added.

Adjective	rapid	gentle	heavy
Adverb	rapidly	gently	heavily

Identifying Adverbs

Underline all the adverbs in each sentence. If there are no adverbs in a sentence, write **None** on the line to the right.

1. If I were very rich, I would travel to Paris.

2. My best friend nearly went to Spain, but, surprisingly, she is afraid of airplanes.

3. Older people frequently travel with tour groups.

4. My mother's job makes her travel too often.

5. The plane left early from Baltimore and landed in New York City.

6. I am rather tired because of the six-hour time change.

7. Because I am so tired, I suggest we stay close to our hotel.

8. I think we should remain indoors in a museum.

9. Some people go through museums slowly, reading every sign.

10. I usually go through museums rather quickly, looking at what is especially beautiful to me.

Name ______________________________ Date ______________

Lesson 4

What Is an Adverb?

More Practice

A. Identifying Adverbs and the Words They Modify

Underline the adverbs in the following sentences. Draw an arrow from each adverb to the word it modifies.

1. Cleo scampered playfully onto my lap.
2. We looked up at the meteor.
3. Kara skimmed the chapter quickly.
4. The doctor has just left his office.
5. We have never visited Salt Lake City.
6. Miko usually leaves her books on the shelf.
7. The movie was rather tedious.
8. The story ended very happily.
9. The teacher seemed unusually cheerful.
10. The summer rain fell extremely heavily.

B. Writing Adverbs

Complete each sentence with an adverb. Write the adverb on the line.

1. When you fly, it's best to arrive at the airport ______________.
2. When I saw the Eiffel Tower, I ______________ ran up to get in line.
3. We found it ______________ difficult to drive on the left side of the road in England.
4. Whenever I visit someplace new, I ______________ take lots of pictures.
5. Even though the plane tickets to China are expensive, I hope to go there ______________.
6. I know that I will be ______________ happy when I see the Grand Canyon.
7. In Hawaii, tourists often spend their time ______________ lying on the beach.
8. If I am not going too far, I ______________ walk, so I can see the sights.
9. In Los Angeles, my friend felt ______________ excited after he saw a movie star.
10. Be ______________ certain that you have a good map in a strange city.

Name ______________________ Date ____________

Lesson 4

What Is an Adverb?

Application

A. Writing Adverbs in Sentences

Use the adverb at the beginning of each item in a sentence.

EXAMPLE soon *The mail carrier should be coming soon.*

1. surprisingly ______________________

2. mournfully ______________________

3. foolishly ______________________

4. sometimes ______________________

5. easily ______________________

6. truly ______________________

7. never ______________________

8. upstairs ______________________

9. nearly ______________________

10. quietly ______________________

B. Writing a Paragraph Using Adverbs

Choose four of the following adverbs to use in a story about a vacation to an exciting city anywhere in the world. Write the story on the lines below. Underline each of these adverbs and any other adverbs that you use in your story.

busily	very	desperately	suddenly	totally
quickly	extremely	nearly	soon	never

CHAPTER 5

Name ______________________________ Date ______________

Lesson 5 Making Comparisons *Teaching*

Adjectives and adverbs may be used to compare people or things. Special forms of these words are used to make comparisons.

Use the **comparative** form of an adjective or adverb when you compare a person or thing with one other person or thing. Use the **superlative** form of an adjective or adverb when you compare someone or something with more than one other person or thing.

Comparative The sun is closer to Earth than any other star.
Superlative The sun is the closest star to Earth.

For most **one-syllable** modifiers, add *-er* to form the comparative (*young, younger*) and *-est* to form the superlative (*old, oldest*).

You can also add *-er* and *-est* to some **two-syllable** adjectives. With others, and with two-syllable adverbs, use the words *more* and *most* (*more careful, most calmly*).

To form the comparative or superlative form of most modifiers with **three syllables,** use the words *more* and *most* (*more dangerous, most dangerous; more clumsily, most clumsily*).

Be sure to use only one sign of comparison at a time (*harder,* not *more harder*).

The comparative and superlative forms of some adjectives and adverbs are formed in irregular ways: *good, better, best; bad, worse, worst; well, better, best; much, more, most; little, less, least.*

A. Identifying Comparative and Superlative Modifiers

On the line, label the boldfaced modifier **C** for comparative, or **S** for superlative.

CHAPTER 5

1. Planets are the **largest** heavenly bodies that orbit the sun. ______
2. Asteroids, meteoroids, and comets are **smaller** than the planets. ______
3. With their improved telescopes, scientists can study the planets **more carefully** than ever before. ______
4. Mercury is the planet **nearest** to the sun. ______
5. Pluto is usually the planet **farthest** from the sun. ______
6. Venus takes **less** time to circle the sun than Uranus does. ______
7. The atmosphere of Venus is about 90 times **heavier** than is Earth's. ______
8. Of all the planets, Saturn has the **most** satellites or moons. ______
9. Jupiter rotates **more quickly** than Mars. ______
10. Although several planets have rings, Saturn has the **most famous** ones. ______

Name ______________________________ Date ______________

Lesson 5

Making Comparisons

More Practice

A. Using Comparisons

Underline the correct form of comparison for each sentence.

1. Of all the objects in our solar system, the moon is (nearer, nearest) to Earth.
2. Because the moon is so close to Earth, it looks (bigger, biggest) than the sun to us.
3. Actually, the sun is 400 times (larger, largest) than the moon.
4. Eclipses of the moon were (more frightening, most frightening) to ancient people than they are to us.
5. Modern people understand astronomy (better, best) than the ancients did.
6. The (more important, most important) surface features of the moon are its craters.
7. Craters caused by meteorites are (smaller, smallest) than those formed by comets or asteroids.
8. Because the moon is so close to Earth, spacecraft can reach the moon (more easily, most easily) than they can reach any planet.
9. Probably the (more exciting, most exciting) event in 1969 was when American astronaut Neil Armstrong landed on the moon.

B. Using Modifiers in Comparisons

After each sentence, write either the comparative or the superlative form of the word in parentheses, depending on what the sentence calls for.

1. Smiling requires (few) muscles than frowning. ______________
2. Is Detroit (far) from here than Traverse City is? ______________
3. These photographs developed (good) than those. ______________
4. The days seem (cold) now than last week. ______________
5. In many cartoons, cats are birds' (bad) enemies. ______________
6. Was Merlin the (wise) of all wizards? ______________
7. Mr. Burr works (hard) than any salesperson at Doe Tools. ______________
8. Diana circles the bases (quickly) than any other player. ______________
9. Our team practices (regularly) than any other team in the league. ______________
10. The hurricane caused (little) damage than the weather forecasters had predicted. ______________

Name ______________________________ Date ______________

Lesson 5

Making Comparisons

Application

A. Proofreading

Proofread the following paragraph. Look especially for comparison errors in adjectives and adverbs. If a sentence contains an error, rewrite it correctly on the line with the same number. If it is correct, write **Correct** on the line.

Meteorites are pieces of meteoroids that reach the earth. **(1)** The most heaviest meteorite found so far is in Namibia, Africa. **(2)** It weighs about 66 tons, which is most weighty than one discovered in Greenland by explorer Robert. E. Peary. **(3)** Canada probably can claim the more enormous meteorite crater in the world. **(4)** At 400 miles across, the depression is wider by far than any other meteorite crater. **(5)** Canada has four other craters, each one biggest than Meteor Crater in Arizona. **(6)** When a huge meteorite crashed to Earth in Siberia many years ago, people nearly 500 miles away saw its light more brighter than the sun. **(7)** The worse damage it did was to destroy many forests and scorch an area 20 miles wide.

1. ______________________________

2. ______________________________

3. ______________________________

4. ______________________________

5. ______________________________

6. ______________________________

7. ______________________________

CHAPTER 5

B. Using Comparisons in Writing

Picture a night of stargazing. Suppose you have decided to look for constellations, planets, or shooting stars, or you simply want to study the moon. Write a paragraph about your experiences, using the comparative or superlative forms of at least five of the adjectives and adverbs below. Underline the forms you use.

eagerly	cold	carefully	good	black
dark	warm	loudly	bad	well
brightly	cool	suddenly	mysterious	little

____

____

____

____

____

Name ______________________ Date ______________

Lesson 6

Adjective or Adverb?

Teaching

Some pairs of adjectives and adverbs are often a source of confusion and mistakes.

Good or Well

Good is always an adjective; it modifies a noun or pronoun. *Well* is an adverb when it modifies a verb, adverb, or adjective and means "skillfully" or "thoroughly." *Well* is an adjective when it refers to your health.

Adjective Today is a good day for a soccer game.
I hope the goalie feels well enough to play.
Adverb Our team should play well today.

Real or Really

Real is always an adjective; it modifies a noun or pronoun. *Really* is always an adverb; it modifies a verb, adverb, or adjective.

Adjective It was a real surprise that we won the last game.
Adverb This is a really enthusiastic crowd, isn't it?

Bad or Badly

Bad is always an adjective; it modifies a noun or pronoun. *Badly* is always an adverb; it modifies a verb, adverb, or adjective.

Adjective That was a bad call.
Adverb He played badly last half.

Using the Correct Adjective or Adverb

Underline the correct modifier from those given in parentheses.

1. The sport that I (real, really) enjoy is soccer.
2. I am the goalie on the team, and I think I am a (good, well) one.
3. In fact, everyone on our team has been playing (good, well) this season.
4. We have a couple of forwards that can run (real, really) fast.
5. Our defensive players have (real, really) powerful kicks.
6. Overall, this season has been going (good, well) for us.
7. In the first game our sweeper took a (bad, badly) fall.
8. Luckily, he felt (good, well) enough to resume playing.
9. We have been playing so (good, well) that we may have a (real, really) chance to make it to the finals.
10. I have been practicing (real, really) hard.
11. I feel so (bad, badly) when I let in a goal.
12. We cannot afford to play (bad, badly) in any game.
13. Making it to the finals is a (real, really) challenge.
14. But, win or lose, this team always has a (good, well) time.

Name ______________________________ Date ______________

Lesson 6

Adjective or Adverb?

More Practice

A. Using the Correct Modifier

Underline the correct word in parentheses in each sentence. Label each word you choose as **ADJ** for adjective or **ADV** for adverb.

1. Stretch your muscles (good, well) before running. ________

2. The pizza with pineapple tastes (good, well). ________

3. Mark felt so (badly, bad) after gym class that he went to the nurse. ________

4. The truck driver drove (real, really) slowly so he could read the addresses. ________

5. If your handwriting is (bad, badly), why don't you enter your paper into the computer? ________

6. The bird was perfectly (good, well) after its wing healed. ________

7. I was sorry to hear that the interview went (bad, badly) for you. ________

8. That soup smells really (well, good), doesn't it? ________

B. Writing with Adjectives and Adverbs

Decide if adjectives and adverbs are used correctly in the following sentences. If you find an error, rewrite the sentence on the line. If the sentence is correct, write **Correct** on the line.

1. Yesterday, the field was real wet.

____

2. We did not play our game because there was a real chance of the players getting hurt bad if they slipped on the wet grass.

____

____

3. Today, the field has dried out real good, and we can play.

____

4. One of the other team's forwards behaved bad and received a yellow card.

____

5. That player just made a really good corner kick.

____

6. Our goalie always feels badly when he misses a real easy shot.

____

Name ______________________ Date ____________

Lesson 6

Adjective or Adverb?

Application

A. Writing Sentences Using Adjectives and Adverbs Correctly

Write sentences using the adjectives and adverbs given.

1. good ______________________

2. well (adverb) ______________________

3. well (adjective) ______________________

4. bad ______________________

6. badly ______________________

7. real ______________________

8. really ______________________

B. Using Adjectives and Adverbs Correctly

Read the conversation below. It contains several errors in the use of *good, well, real, really, bad,* and *badly*. Underline any errors you find. Then rewrite the conversation correctly on the lines below.

"The game today should be real good," said Alex. "I have never seen these two teams play bad."

"Both teams have some real strong players with some good skills," replied Katie. "The goalies play particularly good."

"Haven't you heard? Fernando was injured real bad in the last game. We are all hoping that he will be doing good soon. Everyone feels badly that he will miss today's game."

"That's really bad news. We'll just have to see if his team can play as good without him."

____

____

____

____

____

____

____

____

____

CHAPTER 5

Name ______________________________ Date ______________

Lesson 7

Avoiding Double Negatives

Teaching

A **negative** is a word that implies that something does not exist or happen.

Common Negative Words

barely	never	none	nothing	can't
hardly	no	no one	nowhere	don't
neither	nobody	not	scarcely	hasn't

If two negative words are used where only one is needed, the result is a **double negative.** Avoid double negatives in your speaking and writing.

Nonstandard Hardly no one believes me when I tell my story.
Standard No one believes me when I tell my story. *or* Hardly anyone believes me when I tell my story.

A. Recognizing the Correct Use of Negatives

Circle the letter of the sentence from each pair that uses negatives correctly.

1. a. I wasn't looking for no trouble that night.
b. I wasn't looking for any trouble that night.

2. a. I could hardly believe my eyes when I saw the space ship.
b. I couldn't hardly believe my eyes when I saw the space ship.

3. a. I can't understand anything the aliens are saying.
b. I can't understand nothing the aliens are saying.

4. a. Nobody never expects to be taken aboard an alien ship.
b. Nobody ever expects to be taken aboard an alien ship.

CHAPTER 5

B. Avoiding Double Negatives

Underline the word in parentheses that correctly completes each sentence.

1. I had never seen (no, any) aliens before that strange night.
2. At first, my friend and I didn't see (anything, nothing) unusual in the sky.
3. You wouldn't (ever, never) guess what happened around nine o'clock.
4. When a spaceship landed, I (could, couldn't) scarcely believe it myself.
5. I had never believed (anyone, no one) who said he or she saw an alien.
6. Yet, there it was, looking at me and making gestures that I couldn't (ever, never) understand, as if it was trying to communicate.
7. I was confused, and my friend couldn't make out what the little creature was saying (neither, either).
8. In scarcely (no, any) time at all, the alien climbed back in its ship and disappeared.
9. I never told (nobody, anybody) that I saw the alien that night.
10. I can see that you (can, can't) hardly stop yourself from laughing, but I swear it's all true.

Name ____________________ Date ____________

Lesson 7

Avoiding Double Negatives

More Practice

A. Using the Correct Modifier

Underline the correct word in parentheses in each sentence.

1. I haven't heard of (none, any) of those songs you mentioned.
2. You (haven't, have) never been to a concert?
3. She can't go (anywhere, nowhere) without taking her cell phone.
4. The doctor (hasn't, has) scarcely even touched you with the needle.
5. Haven't you been to the new museum yet (neither, either)?
6. When I turned around I didn't see (no one, anyone) behind me.
7. People in some parts of the United States haven't (ever, never) seen snow.
8. He (could, couldn't) hardly see the performance from where he was sitting.
9. My brother can't drive (nowhere, anywhere) without getting himself lost.

B. Avoiding Double Negatives

Rewrite each sentence to avoid double negatives.

1. There wasn't no one else around when the spaceship landed.

 ____

2. I discovered that I understood the alien even though it wasn't making no sound.

 ____

 ____

3. I hadn't never seen a creature so strange before.

 ____

4. I don't think I can hardly describe the inside of the spaceship.

 ____

5. The glowing metal control panel wasn't like nothing I'd ever seen on Earth.

 ____

 ____

Name ______________________ Date ______________

Lesson 7

Avoiding Double Negatives

Application

A. Avoiding Double Negatives

Choose one word from each pair of words to complete each sentence below. Be sure to avoid double negatives. Cross out each word pair after you have chosen your word.

anything/ nothing	any/ no	anyone/ no one
can/ can't	had/ hadn't	ever/ never

1. I was disappointed when I didn't see ____________ about aliens on the TV news.

2. The police never had ____________ reports about unusual activity that night.

3. I ____________ never been so scared as when I saw that alien.

4. I never told ____________ about my experience on the alien ship.

5. I can't ____________ describe my surprise at being taken aboard.

6. I ____________ scarcely picture sharing our planet with an alien life form.

B. Revising a Paragraph with Double Negatives

The following paragraph contains several double negatives. Read each sentence and decide if it has a double negative. If it does, rewrite it correctly on the corresponding line below. If it is correct, write Correct on the corresponding line.

(1) My sister hasn't never missed an alien movie. **(2)** She loves anything alien, and you can't scarcely see her bedroom wall because of all the alien-related posters. **(3)** However, she doesn't like it when the aliens are portrayed unjustly as evil. **(4)** She would love to become a scientist and try to prove that people haven't nothing to fear from aliens. **(5)** I don't believe aliens want to take over our planet or destroy our kind neither. **(6)** In fact, no one can't really prove anything about aliens at all yet. **(7)** My sister and I know that some people don't believe in the existence of aliens. **(8)** Even so, we won't let nobody stop us from enjoying stories about extraterrestrial life.

1. ______________________________

2. ______________________________

3. ______________________________

4. ______________________________

5. ______________________________

6. ______________________________

7. ______________________________

8. ______________________________

CHAPTER 5

Name ______________________________ Date ____________

Lesson 1

What Is a Preposition?

Teaching

A preposition is a word used to show a relationship between a noun or pronoun and some other word in the sentence.

The dog is **under** the bed. (*under* shows the relationship between *dog* and *bed*)

Common Prepositions				
about	at	despite	like	to
above	before	down	near	toward
across	behind	during	of	under
after	below	except	off	until
against	beneath	for	on	up
along	beside	from	out	with
among	between	in	over	within
around	beyond	inside	past	without
as	by	into	through	

A **prepositional phrase** consists of a preposition, its object, and any modifiers of the object. The **object of the preposition** is the noun or pronoun following the preposition.

People communicate in many ways. (The preposition is *in,* the object of the preposition is *ways,* and the prepositional phrase is *in many ways.*)

Sometimes the same word can be used as a preposition or as an adverb. If there is no object, the word is an adverb.

Adverb Come along.
Preposition The messages travel along the telephone wire.

A. Finding Prepositions and Their Objects

Underline the prepositions in each sentence. Underline the objects of the prepositions twice.

1. People enjoy talking with one another.
2. They share news of their daily lives.
3. News about international events are broadcast on television.
4. Many people find current news on the Internet.
5. Communication methods have changed over the centuries.
6. Sending messages around the globe has become commonplace.

B. Recognizing Prepositions and Adverbs

Decide whether the boldfaced word is a preposition or an adverb. Write **P** on the line if it is a preposition. Write **A** if it is an adverb.

1. I have spoken to you **before,** haven't I? ______
2. **Before** the speech, the audience was restless. ______
3. Get you words **down** on paper before you forget them. ______
4. The train continued **down** the track. ______

Name ______________________________ Date ______________

Lesson 1

What Is a Preposition?

More Practice

A. Identifying Prepositions and Their Objects

Underline each preposition once. Circle the object of the preposition. Sentences may have more than one prepositional phrase.

1. Some of the construction crew built a scaffold near the tower.
2. The library will hold the book until tomorrow.
3. The prompter sat behind the scenery with a small flashlight.
4. Chirps of the newly hatched chicks could be heard in the corridor.
5. A plane made an emergency landing in a cornfield.
6. The elephants lumbered past us toward the water hole.
7. The puppy came into our tent and slept at the foot of my sleeping bag.
8. A skywriter flew over the field during the game.
9. The city was without power for several hours.
10. The cross-country team ran down the avenue and through the park.

B. Recognizing Prepositions and Adverbs

Decide whether the boldfaced word is an adverb or a preposition. Write *Adverb* or *Preposition* on the line.

1. The Pony Express got the mail **through.** ______________
2. The company moved some employees **around.** ______________
3. The ferry passed **under** the bridge. ______________
4. We looked **across** at the crowd on the opposite shore. ______________
5. The circus parade just went **past.** ______________
6. The investigators found clues **inside** the closet. ______________
7. The swimmer held his breath when he went **under.** ______________
8. Ellen saw the bus coming and raced **out** the door. ______________
9. The parade had never passed this way **before.** ______________
10. The horses trotted **around** the ring. ______________
11. A professional doesn't leave her tools lying **around.** ______________
12. The boomerang flew **across** the back yard. ______________

Name ______________________ Date ____________

Lesson 1

What Is a Preposition?

Application

A. Writing with Prepositional Phrases

Add one or more prepositional phrases to each simple sentence. Write your new sentence on the line.

1. The telephone rang.

____

2. The radio announcer reported.

____

3. A television special report aired.

____

4. The telegram arrived.

____

5. Flora wrote a letter.

____

B. Writing with Prepositional Phrases

Use three of these prepositional phrases in an original story. Write your story on the lines below.

by a citizen	with concern	from other countries
to the mayor	around the park	before the election
in the newspaper	across the city	toward the future

____

____

____

____

____

____

____

____

____

____

____

CHAPTER 6

Name ______________________ Date ____________

Lesson 2 Using Prepositional Phrases

Teaching

A **prepositional phrase** is always related to another word in a sentence. It modifies the word in the same way an adjective or adverb does.

An **adjective phrase** is a prepositional phrase that modifies a noun or a pronoun. It can tell *which one, how many,* or *what kind.*

> The capital of the United States is Washington, D.C. (The phrase of the *United States* modifies the noun *capital.*)

An **adverb phrase** is a prepositional phrase that modifies a verb, an adjective, or another adverb. It usually tells *where, when, how, why,* or *to what extent.*

Modifying a verb	Many Americans travel in the summer. (The phrase *in the summer* modifies the verb *travel* telling *when.*)
Modifying an adjective	New York City is remarkable for its public buildings. (The phrase *for its public buildings* modifies the adjective *remarkable.*)
Modifying an adverb	The street system works well for such an old plan. (The phrase *for such an old plan* modifies the adverb *well.*)

Placement of Prepositional Phrases Place the prepositional phrase close to the word it modifies, so you don't confuse your readers.

Confusing	Excited tourists walk down the mall with ice cream bars.
Better	Excited tourists with ice cream bars walk down the mall.

Identifying Prepositional Phrases

Underline the prepositional phrase in each sentence. If it is an adjective phrase, write **ADJ** on the line to the right. If it is an adverb phrase, write **ADV.**

1. The capital of a country should be a beautiful city.
2. Any visitor to Washington, D.C., will see that it is, indeed, beautiful.
3. Visitors are impressed by its broad avenues.
4. The President lives at 1600 Pennsylvania Avenue.
5. The White House is an impressive residence with lovely rose gardens.
6. The national mall was built near the White House.
7. The tall Washington Monument appears on the mall.
8. The Lincoln Memorial with its brooding statue is thought provoking and peaceful.
9. Cherry trees around the Tidal Basin are colorful and inspiring.
10. The Capitol is the home of the United States Congress.

CHAPTER 6

Name ______________________ Date ______________

Lesson 2

Using Prepositional Phrases

More Practice

A. Identifying Prepositional Phrases

In each sentence, underline the word modified by the boldfaced prepositional phrase. On the blank, write **ADJ** or **ADV** to identify what kind of prepositional phrase it is.

1. The actors gathered **around the director.** ______
2. In the science classroom, there are many books **on wildlife.** ______
3. The raging fire spread **over the river** and through the trees. ______
4. **Until next week** the paintings will be on sale at a hotel near Tulsa. ______
5. Music **from the auditorium** could be heard across the hall. ______
6. The oak trees behind the school were sprayed **in the spring.** ______
7. The plant on the windowsill thrives **in the sun.** ______
8. The car came **down the street** and parked outside our house. ______
9. The model airplane **in my brother's room** was made in Germany. ______
10. The monkeys ran from the sound **of humans.** ______

B. Placing Prepositional Phrases

Rewrite each sentence, changing the position of one or more prepositional phrases so that the sentence is no longer confusing.

Example In a big hurry, we saw the senator rush away.
We saw the senator rush away in a big hurry.

1. The tourists with a special display visited the museum.

____

2. Karen sent her father in a sturdy box a souvenir.

____

3. I took a picture of the president with my new camera.

____

4. The tour bus with its beautiful flowers passed the national garden.

____

5. My father beyond the monument parked the car.

____

CHAPTER 6

Name ______________________ Date ______________

Lesson 2

Using Prepositional Phrases

Application

A. Revising Sentences with Misplaced Prepositional Phrases

Rewrite each sentence, changing the position of one or more prepositional phrases so that the sentence is no longer confusing.

EXAMPLE Below the waves we watched the sun sink.
We watched the sun sink below the waves.

1. We waited for the bus inside the mall.

____

2. Behind the clouds we saw the sun disappear.

____

3. Alonzo was walking his dog in his school sweater.

____

4. Inside a tube, Kathy sent her mother a poster.

____

5. The cook with a sour smell threw away the milk.

____

B. Using Prepositional Phrases as Adjectives and Adverbs

Add a prepositional phrase to each sentence. The type of phrase to add is indicated in parentheses after the sentence.

1. The city is the U.S. government center. (Add an adjective phrase.)

____

2. The president spoke to reporters. (Add an adverb phrase.)

____

3. The Secret Service checked the dining room. (Add an adverb phrase.)

____

4. Supporters cheered the president. (Add an adjective phrase.)

____

5. Cars were parked at the curb. (Add an adjective phrase.)

____

Name ______________________________ Date ______________

Lesson 3

Conjunctions

Teaching

A **conjunction** is a word used to join words or groups of words. Different kinds of conjunctions do different jobs.

A **coordinating conjunction** connects words or groups of words used in the same way. The words joined may be used as subjects, objects, predicates, or any other sentence part.

Some common coordinating conjunctions are *and, but, or, nor,* and *yet.* Use *and* to connect similar things or ideas. Use *but* or *yet* to contrast things or ideas. Use *or* or *nor* to introduce a choice.

> Meriwether Lewis and John Clark led an expedition to the West.
> The United States owned the Louisiana Territory but knew little else about it.
> No one had followed the Missouri or the Columbia rivers to their source.

Correlative conjunctions are pairs of conjunctions that connect words used in the same way.

Common correlative conjunctions are *both . . . and, either . . . or, neither . . . nor, not only . . . but also,* and *whether . . . or.*

> Both Lewis and Clark had served in the U.S. Army.

Identifying Conjunctions

Underline all the conjunctions in the following sentences. Remember there are two parts to a correlative conjunction.

1. President Jefferson was looking for a water route between the Atlantic and the Pacific oceans.
2. No one knew whether that was possible or not.
3. Both Lewis and Clark brought their special skills to the expedition.
4. Lewis knew about plants and animals, and Clark was a good mapmaker.
5. Most encounters with Native Americans were friendly, but some were filled with danger.
6. Both the beauty of the land and its abundant wildlife impressed the explorers.
7. The expedition could follow either the right branch of the river or the left one.
8. The explorers needed an interpreter, and they met Sacagawea, a Shoshone woman.
9. The party crossed the mountains and spent the winter in Oregon.
10. Neither Lewis nor Clark should ever be forgotten.
11. We couldn't all be on this expedition, but we can read about it in the explorers' journals.

Name ______________________________ Date ______________

Lesson 3

Conjunctions

More Practice

A. Identifying Conjunctions

In the following sentences, underline the conjunctions.

1. I like hockey, but I prefer football.
2. Neither the coaches nor the timekeepers knew the score.
3. Junk food may taste good, but it is not good for you.
4. Both badminton and volleyball require a net on the court.
5. Jon hit a home run and won the game.
6. The keys are either on the table or in the drawer.
7. Should we play chess or watch the game?
8. Not only was it raining, but it was also hailing.
9. This restaurant serves neither breakfast nor lunch.
10. This pineapple juice is both cool and refreshing.

B. Using Conjunctions

Complete each of the following sentences with a coordinating conjunction or a correlative conjunction.

EXAMPLE Exploring is exciting, ___but___ it is also dangerous.

1. Lewis __________ Clark explored the West, __________ their story is fascinating.
2. __________ Lewis __________ Clark had ever been to Montana before.
3. They thought they knew what they might find, __________ they were still amazed.
4. They took __________ a keelboat __________ canoes up the Missouri River.
5. At one point, they couldn't decide __________ to follow one stream __________ another.
6. They must have made the right choice, __________ we would never have heard about them.
7. If __________ Lewis __________ Clark had been less curious, the United States might not extend to the Pacific coast.
8. On the way back from Oregon, Lewis went one way __________ Clark went through the Yellowstone area.
9. We read about their adventures, __________ reading is not as exciting as exploring.
10. I sometimes wonder __________ I would have gone on this expedition __________ stayed home.

CHAPTER 6

Name ____ Date ________________

Lesson 3

Conjunctions

Application

A. Proofreading

Proofread the following paragraph, adding appropriate conjunctions where they are needed.

Without the help of a Shoshone woman, the Lewis ____________ Clark expedition might have failed. Sacagawea was very young, ____________ she was still able to serve as guide and interpreter for the explorers. Sacagawea had been captured by an enemy tribe when she was only 14 years old ____________ taken from her home. Later she met her husband, a fur trader named Toussaint. Soon after her first baby's birth, ____________ she ____________ Toussaint were hired by Lewis and Clark to guide them through the mountains ____________ act as interpreters to tribes along the way. The trip across the mountains was going to be hard and dangerous, especially without fresh supplies. Imagine Sacagawea's surprise when the weary expedition met a tribe, ____________ its chief was her own brother! ____________ she ____________ her brother had seen each other for years. Sacagawea's brother traded with the expedition for food ____________ supplies. The explorers were able to go on ____________ earn their place in history.

B. Writing with Conjunctions

Imagine that you had been on the Lewis and Clark expedition into the unknown West in 1804. What sights might you have seen? What would have impressed you the most—the wide prairies, the rushing rivers, the steep mountains, or the peaceful ocean? Write a journal entry for one day in your imagined trip. Use at least two coordinating conjunctions and two correlative conjunctions. Underline all the conjunctions.

____

____

____

____

____

____

____

CHAPTER 6

Name ______________________ Date ______________

Lesson 4 Interjections

Teaching

An **interjection** is a word or short phrase used to express emotion, such as *wow* and *my goodness.*

> Hey, that ball was foul!
> Fantastic! That ball is out of here!

Identifying Interjections

Read each sentence. If it contains an interjection, write the interjection on the line to the right. If it does not contain an interjection, write **None** on the line.

1. Wow! It is hot in the sun! ______________
2. Have you been to many games this year? ______________
3. Well, thanks for inviting me along. ______________
4. That's Sammy Sosa himself, isn't it? Awesome! ______________
5. Boy, I wish they would start the game. ______________
6. Finally! Let's stand for the national anthem. ______________
7. Now, let the game begin! ______________
8. Amazing! That ball went 400 yards! ______________
9. Yeah! He struck out all three batters! ______________
10. Gosh! That ball is coming straight at me! ______________
11. Congratulations! You caught the ball! ______________
12. That will be a great souvenir for my collection. ______________
13. Who feels hungry now? ______________
14. Yum! Those tacos look tempting! ______________
15. Whew! If that ball had been fair, we would have lost the game! ______________
16. Hurray! We won! ______________

Name ______________________ Date ______________

Lesson 4

Interjections

More Practice

A. Identifying Interjections

Read each sentence. If it contains an interjection, write the interjection on the line to the right. If it does not contain an interjection, write **None** on the line.

1. Wow! Your serve is so fast today! ______________
2. Well, I have been working with a tennis pro. ______________
3. He gave me some useful pointers for improving my serve. ______________
4. Great! Now I'll never beat you! ______________
5. Ridiculous! Your serve is good too. ______________
6. Hey, I just had a great idea. ______________
7. We could play doubles and challenge two other players. ______________
8. Right! The coach was looking for doubles players. ______________
9. Frankly, I think doubles might be more fun than singles anyway. ______________
10. Excellent! Let's start practicing. ______________

B. Using Interjections

Write an interjection before each of these sentences.

EXAMPLE ____Yuck!____ I wouldn't eat that if I were you!

1. ______________, that coat looks great.
2. ______________! This cocoa is too hot to drink!
3. ______________! We got a touchdown!
4. ______________! Your garden is lovely.
5. ______________, who put the empty milk carton back into the refrigerator?
6. ______________! I forgot my homework!
7. ______________! That cake was absolutely delicious!
8. ______________, that's the way things go sometimes.
9. ______________! My parachute hasn't opened yet!
10. ______________! I'm so proud of you!

Name ______________________ Date ____________

Lesson 4

Interjections

Application

A. Writing Sentences with Interjections

Write a sentence for each of these interjections. You can decide for yourself whether to use a comma or an exclamation point after the interjection. An exclamation point after an interjection shows stronger emotion than a comma does.

Example yikes *Yikes! My brakes aren't working!*

1. yum ______________________
2. hooray ______________________
3. ouch ______________________
4. gee ______________________
5. hey ______________________
6. eek ______________________
7. wow ______________________
8. golly ______________________
9. whew ______________________
10. well ______________________

B. Writing a Conversation with Interjections

Suppose you were at a sporting event such as a football, baseball, basketball, or soccer game with a friend. You would probably use quite a few interjections as you reacted to what was happening in the game. Write a conversation between two fans who are watching a game. Use at least four interjections whenever one of the speakers expresses strong emotion.

____

____

____

____

____

____

____

____

CHAPTER 6

Name ______________________________ Date ______________

Lesson 1

Gerunds and Gerund Phrases

Teaching

A **verbal** is a word that is formed from a verb but acts as a noun, an adjective, or an adverb.

A **gerund** is a verbal that ends in *–ing* and acts as a noun. A **gerund phrase** consists of the gerund with its modifiers and complements.

Painting a landscape requires careful observation. (The gerund is *painting*.)

In sentences, gerunds and gerund phrases may be used any place that nouns may be used.

As subject	Painting is my favorite pastime.
As predicate nominative	My favorite pastime is painting portraits. (phrase)
As direct object	I love painting with watercolors. (phrase)
As object of a preposition	I get in touch with nature by painting.

A. Finding Gerunds and Gerund Phrases

In each sentence, underline every gerund phrase once. Underline each gerund twice.

1. Painting still-life pictures taught Mike a lot about color.
2. Studying art also taught him about history.
3. His main goal is improving his brushwork.
4. Creating art is hard work but also lots of fun.
5. Martina started painting with oils this year.
6. People like visiting art galleries.

B. Identifying Gerunds and Gerund Phrases

Underline each gerund or gerund phrase. On the blank, write how it is used: **S** for subject, **PN** for predicate nominative, **DO** for direct object, or **OP** for object of a preposition.

1. Painting made me appreciate how light affects color. ______
2. John prefers taking photos of people. ______
3. We encouraged his entering the competition. ______
4. Mom kept me from going without my jacket. ______
5. Dorie's best subject is acting in drama class. ______
6. Finding the right tool is half the job. ______
7. After jogging, Mr. Conway loved to eat doughnuts. ______
8. The problem is thinking of a good topic. ______
9. Do you remember fingerpainting in kindergarten? ______
10. Jonathan got paid for sculpting the dolphin. ______

Name ______________________ Date ____________

Lesson 1

Gerunds and Gerund Phrases

More Practice

A. Identifying Gerunds and Gerund Phrases

Underline each gerund or gerund phrase. In the blank, write how it is used: **S** for subject, **PN** for predicate nominative, **DO** for direct object, or **OP** for object of a preposition.

1. For a crisp texture, avoid overcooking the vegetables. ______
2. Before running, Jim always stretches. ______
3. Omar preferred watching the hockey game. ______
4. For Joanna, making a papier-mâché globe was a messy project. ______
5. Marcello's specialty is sculpting. ______
6. Collecting candy on Halloween still appeals to Del. ______
7. Noreen hates being left behind. ______
8. Thomas really dislikes drawing. ______
9. Aunt Frances started searching the attic for baby clothes. ______
10. My dog's only trick is singing. ______

B. Using Gerunds and Gerund Phrases

Rewrite each sentence. Change the boldfaced word or words to a gerund or gerund phrase. Underline each gerund. You may need to alter some other words in the sentence.

1. **To paint landscapes well** has always been Juan's goal.

____

2. After **he took lessons,** Juan showed great improvement.

____

3. His goal for this year is **to sell at least one of his works.**

____

4. He feels that **to make a sale** will prove he has some ability.

____

5. We say he should be happy with **his creation of a decent picture.**

____

CHAPTER 7

Name ______________________ Date ______________

Lesson 1

Gerunds and Gerund Phrases

Application

A. Using Gerunds and Gerund Phrases

Write sentences using the following gerunds and gerund phrases in the sentence parts indicated.

1. painting by numbers (subject) ______________________

2. sculpting in marble (object of preposition) ______________________

3. sketching cartoons (predicate noun) ______________________

4. cleaning brushes (direct object) ______________________

5. choosing a good subject (your choice of sentence part) ______________________

B. Using Gerunds and Gerund Phrases in Writing

You are on a committee whose job is to design a model city. What public buildings and parks will be needed, in addition to homes, stores, offices, and factories? What concerns (such as safety, avoiding wasted travel time, and providing good scenery) should be taken into account when locating these different types of buildings? Write a paragraph in which you outline one or more topics that the committee should discuss. Use five or more gerunds in your paragraph.

CHAPTER 7

Name ______________________ Date ______________

Lesson 2 Participles and Participial Phrases

Teaching

A **participle** is a verbal that acts as an adjective. It modifies a noun or pronoun. There are two kinds of participles: present participles and past participles. The **present participle** always ends in *–ing.*

The listening crowd was still. (The present participle *listening* modifies *crowd.*)

The past participle of a regular verb ends in *–ed.* For irregular verbs such as *tell,* the past participle has a different ending.

The amused listeners laughed at the ending. (regular verb.)
That retold story is still funny. (irregular verb.)

A **participial phrase** consists of a participle plus its modifiers and complements.

The crowd, listening to the storyteller, was spellbound. (modifies *crowd.*)
Told in many versions, this story is still funny. (modifies *story.*)

Gerunds, present participles, and progressive verbs all end in *ing.* Here's how to tell them apart.

Participle	What is that **barking** sound?	Can be replaced by an adjective such as "loud"
Gerund	That **barking** is the neighbor's dog.	Can be replaced by a noun such as "noise"
Verb	The dog is **barking** at our cat.	Always preceded by a helping verb

Identifying Participles and Participial Phrases

Underline the participle or participial phrase in each sentence. Underline twice the noun or pronoun that it modifies.

Example: The plane, veering wildly, almost crashed to the ground.

1. The old flag, battered by wind and weather, was finally replaced.
2. Finished, the artists cleaned their brushes.
3. Exhausted, Victor fell to the ground after his long run.
4. The skaters, moving effortlessly, danced across the ice.
5. Crossing the old bridge, she passed the village store and the stable.
6. Nan, breathing deeply, bent her knees and lifted the box.
7. Leaving, Doug promised that he would be back.
8. The postal clerk, hurrying, placed the mail in the wrong place.
9. The promised troops did not arrive until it was too late.
10. The alarmed workers saw smoke and fled the factory.
11. The laughing children dashed onto the playground.
12. Cheering crowds welcomed home the winning team.

CHAPTER 7

Name ______________________________ Date ______________

Lesson 2

Participles and Participial Phrases

More Practice

A. Identifying Participles and Participial Phrases

Underline the participle or participial phrase in each sentence. On the blank to the right, write the word that the participle or participial phrase modifies.

1. The art students, brought by bus, toured the museum. ____________
2. The search party found the skiers huddled together. ____________
3. The antique desk, collecting dust in a corner, is priceless. ____________
4. Holding her torch aloft, the Statue of Liberty welcomes newcomers to the United States. ____________
5. Graduation came at last for the exhausted students. ____________
6. The letter, damaged in the mail, finally reached its destination. ____________
7. Completed in record time, the new building was open for business. ____________
8. The game show contestant, thinking hard about the question, didn't answer in time. ____________
9. We watched the goldfish swimming in the pond. ____________
10. Hiking briskly, we reached the mountain pass at noon. ____________

B. Distinguishing Between Gerunds and Participles

In each sentence, underline the verbal. On the line, label it as either a **Gerund** or a **Participle.** Underline twice the word each participle modifies.

1. Baking is a major project for the holidays. ____________
2. Baking in the oven, the bread smelled delicious. ____________
3. The burgers, sizzling on the grill, were almost ready. ____________
4. Dressing up for parades is a family tradition. ____________
5. The woman, dressed as a princess, has the lead in the play. ____________
6. Seeing the accident, Lori helped the boy to his feet. ____________
7. Seeing the old slides reminded me of the good times we had. ____________
8. Talking is rude while the movie is on. ____________
9. Talking among themselves, the actors missed their cues. ____________
10. The dog, wagging its tail, eyed the steak. ____________
11. Dropping the toy, the baby laughed. ____________
12. Dancing takes strength and discipline. ____________

Name ________________________________ Date ______________

Lesson 2

Participles and Participial Phrases

Application

A. Identifying Participles and Participial Phrases

You are writing a fairy tale about knights, princesses, and fire-breathing dragons. Write sentences for the story using the following participles and participial phrases. (Use a comma after any participial phrase that begins a sentence.) Underline the word modified by each participle or participial phrase.

1. disguised ________________________________

____

2. building a fortress ________________________________

____

3. enraged ________________________________

____

4. threatening the kingdom ________________________________

____

5. determined to save the kingdom ________________________________

____

B. Using Present and Past Participles in Writing

The following story is missing several participles. The verbs that must be used in the participles are listed here. Choose the right verb for each blank, and write either the present participle or the past participle on the line, as needed.

worry	peep	accompany	
pretend	need	trust	defeat

The fox appears in many folktales. A hen, often ______________ by a brood of chicks, is another stock character. ______________ about her chicks, the hen looks for help. ______________ the fox, she doesn't recognize him for what he really is. The hungry fox really wants to eat her and her ______________ brood too. ______________ to be harmless, the fox offers to help the hen out. The hen, ______________ help, takes him up on his offer. Then, suddenly realizing her error, she escapes with her chicks. ______________ at his own game, the fox heads back to his den still hungry.

CHAPTER 7

Name ______________________________ Date ______________

Lesson 3 Infinitives and Infinitive Phrases

Teaching

An **infinitive** is a verb form that usually begins with the word *to* and acts as a noun, an adjective, or an adverb. In each example below, the infinitive is *to eat.* An **infinitive phrase** consists of an infinitive plus its complements and modifiers. The entire phrase functions as a noun, adjective, or adverb.

As noun To eat healthily was Anna's New Year's resolution. (subject)
Anna wanted to eat healthily. (direct object)
Anna's resolution was to eat healthily. (predicate noun)

As adjective Her plan to eat healthily was fine. (*to eat healthily* modifies *plan*)

As adverb To eat healthily, Anna will learn the art of cooking vegetables properly. (*To eat healthily* modifies *will learn,* telling *why.*)

To decide whether a phrase is an **infinitive** or a prepositional phrase, look at the word after *to.* If the word is a verb, the phrase is an infinitive. If the word is a noun, pronoun, or modifier the phrase is a prepositional phrase.

John is going to the library. (prepositional phrase)
Does Marie want to go with him? (infinitive phrase)

A. Identifying Infinitives and Infinitive Phrases

Underline every infinitive.

1. Lola hesitated to order the pork sausage.
2. We don't care to go out for breakfast.
3. Who wants to run to the store for some milk and bread?
4. Marie's idea was to try eating vegetarian twice a week.
5. To keep more taste and food value in vegetables, I use a steamer.
6. Lou's intention to have healthy meals clashed with his love of ice cream.
7. To cook eggs for all ten of us, you'll need a much larger pan.
8. Where can you go to school to learn to be a chef?

B. Identifying Infinitive Phrases

Underline the infinitive phrase in each sentence. On the blank, write how it is used: **N** for noun, **ADJ** for adjective, or **ADV** for adverb.

1. Her suggestion was to leave at 9:00 A.M. ______
2. It was his idea to take a cab instead of the subway. ______
3. To get to the French restaurant, take a right at the next street. ______
4. Colin wants to live forever, but he eats like there's no tomorrow. ______
5. To eat healthily is not enough; you also need regular physical exercise. ______

Name ______________________ Date ______________

Lesson 3

Infinitives and Infinitive Phrases

More Practice

A. Identifying Infinitive Phrases

Underline the infinitive phrase in each sentence. On the blank, write how it is used: **N** for noun, **ADJ** for adjective, or **ADV** for adverb.

1. To have a balanced diet, keep the food triangle in mind. ______
2. George wants to take Lea out tonight. ______
3. Fifty years ago, people didn't know to avoid "bad" cholesterol. ______
4. Would you like to read this detective novel? ______
5. Avoiding green, leafy vegetables is guaranteed to ruin your health. ______
6. To get good food at that place is impossible. ______
7. My grandmother taught me to make lentil soup. ______
8. Brenda went to that popular, crowded cafe simply to see her friends. ______
9. We listened to Rosalie's suggestion to disguise the leftovers. ______
10. Everyone plans to bring a potluck dish to the party. ______

B. Using Infinitive Phrases

Use each of the following infinitive phrases in a sentence.

1. to make soup

____

2. to get to dinner on time

____

3. to ask you to dinner

____

4. to wait tables

____

5. to snack before the TV

____

CHAPTER 7

Name ______________________ Date ______________

Lesson 3

Infinitives and Infinitive Phrases

Application

A. Using Infinitive Phrases

Use each of the following infinitive phrases in a sentence.

1. to eat a balanced diet
____
2. to chew his food slowly
____
3. to teach nutrition
____
4. to avoid high-calorie snacks
____
5. to get enough vitamins
____

B. Writing Infinitive Phrases

Rewrite the following paragraph, changing every sentence to include an infinitive or infinitive phrase.

EXAMPLE Eating well is important to your health.
To eat well is important to your health.

Laying the foundations for health is simple. Your needs include choosing the right foods and exercising. For choosing foods wisely, consider the food pyramid. This guide advises eating some foods from each food group daily. The key is balancing your diet—some high-protein food, some fruits and vegetables, and some bread or pasta. For exercising effectively, stay simple. Walking every day beats going to the gym once a week.

____
____
____
____
____
____
____
____
____

CHAPTER 7

Name ______________________ Date ______________

Lesson 1 What Is a Clause?

Teaching

A **clause** is a group of words that contains both a subject and a verb. There are two kinds of clauses: independent and dependent.

An **independent clause** expresses a complete thought and can stand alone as a sentence. An independent clause is also called a **main clause.**

The gardener calculated the total area.

SUBJECT VERB

A **dependent clause** contains a subject and a verb, but it does not express a complete thought. It cannot stand alone as a sentence. Another name for a dependent clause is a **subordinate clause.** Most dependent clauses are introduced by words like *although, before, because, so that, when, while, so,* and *that.*

after she had measured the plot carefully

A dependent clause can be joined to an independent clause to express a complete thought.

The gardener calculated the total area after she had measured the plot carefully.

Identifying Independent and Dependent Clauses

Identify each boldfaced group of words by writing **IND** for independent clause and **DEP** for dependent clause.

1. **Joyce enjoyed geometry** more than she enjoyed algebra. ______
2. She liked the fact **that the class began with simple shapes.** ______
3. **A point was the first thing** that the students learned about. ______
4. **A point has no length or width.** ______
5. When you study geometry, **you must use terms accurately.** ______
6. For example, you may not say *line* **when you mean *line segment.*** ______
7. A triangle, **which everyone recognizes,** is a shape made of three line segments. ______
8. An equilateral triangle is a triangle **whose three sides are equal.** ______
9. An isosceles triangle is different **because it has only two equal sides.** ______
10. When Nick draws triangles, **he uses a ruler.** ______
11. **Every square is a rectangle,** but not every rectangle is a square. ______
12. What is the reason **why this is true?** ______
13. **There are some statements about shapes** that cannot be proved. ______
14. Statements **that cannot be proved** are called theorems. ______

Name ______________________________ Date ______________

Lesson 1

What Is a Clause?

More Practice

A. Identifying Independent and Dependent Clauses

Identify each boldfaced group of words by writing **IND** for independent clause and **DEP** for dependent clause.

1. The facts **that are taught in math classes** can be useful in practical problems. _____
2. Although Gene wants to paint his room, **he needs to buy paint first.** _____
3. He must figure the wall area **so that he'll buy the right amount of paint.** _____
4. **First he measures the length of each wall and the height of the room.** _____
5. Then he measures the windows and doors, **which do not need to be painted.** _____
6. **Gene calculates the area of the total wall space,** and then he subtracts the area of the windows and doors. _____
7. Most people can do the math easily **when they use calculators or computers.** _____
8. Before you can multiply or subtract, **you must decide which numbers to use.** _____
9. Gene learned the formulas **that he applies** in his grade school math classes. _____
10. He won't waste money **if he measures and calculates correctly.** _____

B. Identifying and Correcting Fragments

This paragraph includes several dependent clauses that are not attached as they should be to independent clauses. Rewrite the paragraph, connecting the dependent clauses to appropriate independent clauses. Rearrange the order of clauses as needed.

When Lindy took up crocheting. She started with a scarf. She chose three colors. That she particularly liked. Directions for the scarf were in a magazine. Lindy decided to make the scarf shorter than the one shown in the magazine. Because she wasn't sure of her ability. The scarf turned out well. When she went on to her next project. Lindy tried gloves. Which required more skill. That project turned out well too.

____

____

____

____

____

____

____

CHAPTER 8

Name ______________________________ Date ______________

Lesson 1

What Is a Clause?

Application

A. Identifying Independent and Dependent Clauses

If an item is a sentence consisting of only one independent clause, write **IND** on the line. If it is a fragment consisting of only a dependent clause, write **DEP**. If the item is a sentence consisting of both an independent and a dependent clause, write either **IND + DEP** or **DEP + IND** to show the order of clauses.

Example After the snow fell. *DEP*

1. We had to leave the party because the room was so crowded. ______

2. Although the competition was rough. ______

3. Daisy drove the yellow car out to her cousin's home in the country. ______

4. Since Beverly's voice is strong, she won the lead in the musical. ______

5. Jeffrey likes music that was written over 300 years ago. ______

6. Because the rain was so heavy. ______

7. Jay asked the store clerk for directions. ______

8. After the bees chased us inside, we watched TV. ______

9. That grew almost six feet tall. ______

10. Dinah read a magazine while she waited for the bus. ______

B. Correcting Fragments

In Exercise A, which items were fragments with the answer DEP? Write the numbers of those items on the lines below. Then complete each item by adding an independent clause to the dependent clause. Write the corrected sentence after the item number.

Example After the snow fell.
After the snow fell, we had a snowball fight.

Revision of # ___ ______________________________

____

Revision of # ___ ______________________________

____

Revision of # ___ ______________________________

____

CHAPTER 8

Name ______________________ Date ______________

Lesson 2

Simple and Compound Sentences

Teaching

A **simple sentence** has one independent clause and no dependent clauses. Even a simple sentence can be elaborate, and it may have compound parts.

Ed and Vi read and compared the essays. (compound subject, compound verb)

A **compound sentence** has two or more independent clauses joined together, but no dependent clauses. The clauses must be close in thought. They may be joined by a comma and a coordinating conjunction or by a semicolon.

They chose Maxine's essay as the winner, **but** the judges said the final choice was hard.

Ed and Vi disagreed on some essays; **however,** they agreed on the quality of Maxine's writing.

The following are coordinating conjunctions:

for and nor or but so yet

Identifying Kinds of Sentences

Identify each sentence below with **S** for simple or **CD** for compound.

1. It was pouring rain; getting a cab was impossible. ______
2. Miguel patched and cleaned the sails of the boat. ______
3. The magazine was both timely and readable. ______
4. Ted read the instructions, and then he built the model. ______
5. At first, television stations were on the air only a few hours a day, but now many broadcast 24 hours a day. ______
6. Computers and printers are standard equipment in most classrooms. ______
7. Leo took the flag down, and Rosaria folded it. ______
8. The train came in early, but I was already at the station. ______
9. The wind started blowing in the morning and kept on until late in the day. ______
10. The storm forced waste water into the lake, so swimming is prohibited today. ______
11. All-electric cars are still too expensive to operate; this hybrid car, however, combines batteries with a gas-powered engine. ______
12. The legendary founders of Rome were raised by wolves. ______
13. Books and clothes were scattered all over the twins' room. ______
14. The picnic begins at noon; the clouds should have cleared by then. ______
15. I finished my homework early and then went outside. ______

Name ______________________________ Date ______________

Lesson 2

Simple and Compound Sentences

More Practice

A. Identifying Kinds of Sentences

Identify each sentence below with **S** for simple or **CD** for compound.

1. Helium weighs more than hydrogen, but it is less dangerous than the lighter gas. ______

2. A severe storm struck the area and downed power lines. ______

3. The students visited a nursing home; most of them enjoyed the experience. ______

4. The rain stopped abruptly, and cold air swept in from the north. ______

5. The stilt-walker fell during his performance, but his only injury was to his pride. ______

6. The electrician needed tools and insulated wire to restore service. ______

7. Marisa doesn't often express opinions; nevertheless, she recommends this book. ______

8. I must have lost the tickets; they aren't in the envelope. ______

9. In the evening Carlos usually studies or reads at the library. ______

10. Astronauts train hard and prepare for the unexpected. ______

B. Combining Sentences

Combine the two sentences in each item to make a compound sentence. Use a semicolon alone, or a comma with one of the coordinating conjunctions: *and, but, or, nor, for, so, yet.*

1. The benefit dinner was a success. The school band still needed more money for new uniforms.

____

____

2. The skater did a back flip. The crowd applauded.

3. Jane's newest house robot moves smoothly. She's very proud of it.

____

4. Mike worked on the car for hours over the weekend. It still sounds loud.

____

____

Name ______________________________ Date ______________

Lesson 2

Simple and Compound Sentences

Application

Combining Sentences

In all but two of these items, the two simple sentences can be combined as a compound sentence. If the sentences are close in thought, combine them using a semicolon alone, or a comma with one of the coordinating conjunctions: *and, but, or, nor, for, so, yet.* If the sentences are not close in thought, write **Unconnected Simple Sentences.**

1. Usually this flight takes an hour. This time it took 90 minutes because of strong winds.

____

____

2. One usher took our tickets at the door. Another guided us to our seats.

____

3. The professor has a strong policy against admitting latecomers to class. The topic of today's lecture was "Shakespeare's Influence on the English Language."

____

____

4. Bob found an old, nicked-up radio at a garage sale. He has restored it beautifully.

____

5. My sister had a babysitting job at 6:30 P.M. We ate dinner early.

____

6. You'll need to get a new flashlight for your hike. The switch on this one is broken.

____

7. I don't feel well today. The year-end sale at Big Sales offers great discounts.

____

8. We had snow on the weekend. It melted quickly afterwards.

____

Name ______________________ Date ______________

Lesson 3 Complex Sentences

Teaching

A **complex sentence** has one independent clause and one or more dependent clauses.

> Although every sport involves some risk, people who take part in extreme sports face a higher-than-average level of risk.

Many dependent clauses are introduced by a subordinating conjunction. A subordinating conjunction relates a dependent clause to an independent clause. Here is a list of common subordinating conjunctions:

after	as soon as	even though	than	until	wherever
although	because	if	though	when	which
as	before	since	unless	whenever	while

A. Understanding Complex Sentences

In each complex sentence below, find and underline one of the following independent clauses. Then underline each dependent clause twice.

My great-aunt rents a condo near the lake.
The falling tree barely missed the house.
Our class president introduced the speaker.

1. When the high winds blew it down, the falling tree barely missed the house.
2. My great-aunt, who is 84, rents a condo near the lake.
3. Our class president introduced the speaker, whose topic was choosing a career.
4. When she is in town each summer, my great-aunt rents a condo near the lake.
5. The falling tree barely missed the house where my cousin lives.
6. Our class president, who is in my home room, introduced the speaker.
7. My great-aunt rents a condo near the lake, which she can see from the balcony.
8. The falling tree, which was toppled by high winds, hit the garage.
9. My great-aunt rents a condo, which is really quite roomy, near the lake.
10. Although she had laryngitis, our class president introduced the speaker.

B. Understanding Complex Sentences

In each of these complex sentences, underline only the independent clause.

1. Although I try, I can't understand the appeal of extreme sports.
2. I saw a program where an extreme skier was interviewed.
3. A videotape, which was part of the program, showed her accident.
4. When she hit a rough spot, she fell and tumbled down the slope.
5. Though she had spent months recovering from her injuries, she wanted to try the slope again.

Name ______________________________ Date ______________

Lesson 3

Complex Sentences

More Practice

A. Understanding Complex Sentences

In each of these complex sentences, underline each independent clause once and each dependent clause twice.

1. Although the heat is on, it is still cold in here.
2. The trip takes an hour unless traffic is heavy.
3. When the music stops, change partners.
4. No one came when we called.
5. Horses can sleep while they stand.
6. When it gets dark, this light will go on automatically.
7. The bread is stale, although we just bought it.
8. No one may enter after the concert has begun.
9. The cashier had trouble when the electricity went out.
10. After the game ends, we'll go for something to eat.

B. Identifying Kinds of Sentences

Identify each sentence below with **S** for simple, **CD** for compound, or **CX** for complex.

1. One of the sports that can be classified as extreme is free diving. ______
2. Participants hold their breath and dive hundreds of feet straight down in the ocean. ______
3. Deep below the ocean, water pressure squeezes the internal organs of divers, and darkness blinds them. ______
4. The return to the surface can kill a diver if he or she comes up too fast. ______
5. When the body doesn't have time to adjust to changing pressure, internal gases expand too fast. ______
6. The sudden expansion of gases causes explosions in arteries. ______
7. Still, the activity is popular with people who like dangerous challenges. ______
8. The free diving federation refuses to recognize records in "no-limits" free diving because that method of diving is too dangerous. ______
9. "Variable-weight" and "constant-weight" free diving are approved methods. ______
10. Scuba divers, who wear oxygen tanks, accompany free divers to help them if problems arise underwater. ______

Name ______________________________ Date ______________

Lesson 3

Complex Sentences

Application

A. Creating Complex Sentences

Combine each numbered sentence with the sentence that follows to make a complex sentence. Write the new sentence on the line provided.

(1) Ice climbing is a dangerous sport. In it, climbers pull themselves up frozen waterfalls. **(2)** The water was falling. It froze. **(3)** Climbers attach sharp pointed metal cleats to their boots. Then they start up. **(4)** The sun warms a frozen waterfall. The waterfall will give way under a climber.

1. ______________________________

2. ______________________________

3. ______________________________

4. ______________________________

B. Revising Complex Sentences

Underline the independent clause in each of these complex sentences. Then rewrite the sentence, keeping the independent clause but supplying a new dependent clause for each of the original dependent clauses.

1. As darkness closed in around the campfire, we all began to shiver.

____

2. The traffic was heavier after the bus reached the downtown streets.

____

3. Although June had just begun, the lake was warm enough for swimming.

____

4. I feel like dancing whenever I hear my favorite song on the radio.

____

CHAPTER 8

Name ______________________________ Date ______________

Lesson 4

Kinds of Dependent Clauses

Teaching

An **adjective clause** is a dependent clause that is used as an adjective. An adjective clause modifies a noun or pronoun. It tells *what kind, which one, how many,* or *how much.*

Gonfalon is a word that I'd never seen outside of this book. (*What kind of word?*)

Adjective clauses are usually joined to the main clause by **relative pronouns** such as *who, whom, whose, that,* and *which.* A clause beginning with *which* is set off by commas.

A gonfalon is a banner that is hung from a crosspiece. (*Which banner?*)

The word, which is Italian, isn't used much these days. (clause not necessary)

An **adverb clause** is a dependent clause that is used as an adverb. It modifies a verb, adjective, or adverb. Adverb clauses tell *where, when, how, why, to what extent,* and *under what condition.*

When I saw the word, I had to look it up. (*When* did I look it up? Modifies verb)

Adverb clauses are usually joined to the main clause by **subordinating conjunctions** such as *if, because, although, as, when, where, since, before,* and *while.* If the adverb clause comes before the independent clause, use a comma after the adverb clause.

A **noun clause** is a dependent clause used as a noun. Noun clauses may be used anywhere in a sentence that nouns can be used. If you can substitute the word *someone* or *something* for a clause in a sentence, it is a noun clause.

Subject	What the word means puzzled me at first.
Direct Object	The dictionary explained what the word means.
Object of a Preposition	I'm no longer confused about what the word means.
Predicate Noun	A banner is what the word means.

Usually, a noun clause is joined to the main clause by words such as *who, whom, whoever, whomever, that, which, what, when, how, where, why,* and *whether.*

Identifying Adjective, Adverb, and Noun Clauses

Write **ADJ** (adjective), **ADV** (adverb), or **N** (noun) to identify each boldfaced clause.

1. Sometimes an unfamiliar word is explained by **how it is used in a passage.** ______
2. **If the context of a word doesn't make its meaning clear,** a dictionary will help. ______
3. An old story may use words **that are no longer in daily use.** ______
4. **What a word means** may change over the years, as well. ______
5. Another complication is **that a word may have different meanings.** ______
6. **When you talk about a square in geometry,** you mean a four-sided figure. ______
7. A person **who is square,** however, is a dull person. ______
8. **How *square* came to refer to a dull person** is not obvious. ______
9. About a century ago, you complimented a person **if you called him or her square.** ______
10. Then, *square* referred to a person **who was fair, honest, and reliable.** ______

CHAPTER 8

Name ______________________ Date ______________

Lesson 4

Kinds of Dependent Clauses

More Practice

A. Identifying Adjective, Adverb, and Noun Clauses

In each sentence, underline the dependent clause. On the line, write **ADJ** (adjective), **ADV** (adverb), or **N** (noun) to identify the clause.

EXAMPLE Writers who use unusual words challenge readers. ADJ

1. One tool that helps you learn about an unfamiliar word is a dictionary. ______
2. If you sit down with a novel and a dictionary, you can refer to the dictionary often. ______
3. Anyone who sits down with a novel and a dictionary is an unusual reader. ______
4. How a word begins and ends often gives clues to its meaning. ______
5. For example, since *amorphous* ends in *-ous,* it is probably an adjective. ______
6. Also, the prefix *a-,* which means "without" or "not," might be helpful. ______
7. Still, what *morph* means remains the critical question. ______
8. If you are familiar with the word *metamorphosis,* you might figure out the meaning of *morph* from that word. ______
9. You might combine the bits of information that you have so far with the context. ______
10. If all else fails, go to the dictionary. ______

B. Identifying Clauses and Their Roles

In each item, underline once the dependent clause. If it is an adjective or adverb clause, underline twice the word it modifies. If it is a noun clause, write **S, O,** or **PN** to tell whether the clause is used as the subject of a verb, direct or indirect object of a verb or object of a preposition, or a predicate noun.

1. Myra looked as if she were really surprised. ______
2. Ask whoever is on the beach to run for help. ______
3. The book that Perry ordered has arrived at the bookstore. ______
4. Danita is saving her old watch for when the new one stops. ______
5. Gordon laughed when he saw his class picture. ______
6. Rhoda always sits in the seat that is closest to the door. ______
7. How the raccoon entered the house was obvious. ______
8. The homework was easier for Tyrone after he reviewed the chapter. ______

Name ______________________________ Date ______________

Lesson 4

Kinds of Dependent Clauses

Application

A. Identifying Adjective, Adverb, and Noun Clauses

Each sentence has at least one dependent clause. Underline each dependent clause, and, above the underlined words, write **ADJ** (adjective), **ADV** (adverb), or **N** (noun) to identify its type.

1. Words that are named after people make me curious about the people. ______
2. It wasn't hard for me to figure out where the word *curie* came from. ______
3. Clearly, *curie,* which means "a unit of radioactivity," is named after Madame Curie. ______
4. When I came across the word *faraday,* I learned that it was named after Michael Faraday. ______
5. Since a faraday is a measure of electricity, I figured that Mr. Faraday must have been a scientist. ______
6. I read an encyclopedia article that tells of his life. ______
7. An *eponym* refers to a person's name that is used to name something else. ______
8. Everyone can guess what was named after the Earl of Sandwich. ______
9. If something is ever named after you, what would you like it to be? ______

B. Using Dependent Clauses

Rewrite each sentence, adding a clause that fits the description in parentheses. Change words in the original sentence as needed.

1. Once upon a time, magicians were as powerful as kings. (Use *when*)

____

____

2. A greedy king built a fort. (Adverb clause; use *where*)

____

3. The castle was crumbling. (Adjective clause; use *where*)

____

4. Someone was forced to serve the king. (Noun clause, subject of *was forced*)

____

5. A magician stopped the king. (Use *who.*)

____

Name ______________________________ Date ______________

Lesson 5

Compound-Complex Sentences

Teaching

A **compound-complex sentence** has two or more independent clauses and one or more dependent clauses.

> (independent clause) For years, nobody had entered the old house, **but** (independent clause) everyone knew the story (dependent clause) that the house was haunted.

A. Identifying Clauses

In the compound-complex sentences below, the dependent clauses are underlined. Identify the sentence parts named in the parentheses, and write them on the line.

1. Many people claimed that they had seen ghosts in the windows, and others believed them.

(simple subject and verb of the dependent clause) ______________________

(simple subject and verb of the second independent clause) ______________________

2. Each night, as the clock strikes midnight, a strong wind blows the front door open, or can you explain its opening in another way?

(simple subject and verb of the first independent clause) ______________________

(simple subject and verb of the second independent clause) ______________________

3. The bank that owns the old building has tried to sell it, but nobody wants to buy it, and no one wants to live near it.

(simple subject and verb of the dependent clause) ______________________

(simple subject and verb of the first independent clause) ______________________

B. Identifying Kinds of Sentences

Identify each sentence below with **CD** for compound, **CX** for complex, or **CD-CX** for compound-complex.

1. Shake the bottle well, but don't spill the juice. ______

2. The message that Alex sent was hard to understand, and help was slow in arriving. ______

3. The garden flourished, with sunflowers and hollyhocks towering above the marigolds, dahlias, and shorter flowers. ______

4. At the end of the concert, audience members jumped to their feet, and enthusiastic applause broke out. ______

5. As temperatures dropped close to freezing, many orange groves were threatened. ______

6. The guide who escorted our group spoke three languages, so we had no problems. ______

CHAPTER 8

Name ______________________________ Date ______________

Lesson 5 Compound-Complex Sentences

More Practice

A. Identifying Clauses

In each compound-complex sentence below, draw parentheses around each independent clause and underline each dependent clause.

1. When the campfire was burning steadily, all the campers sat on the ground around it, and someone began to tell a scary story.
2. The story was not very good; however, because the campers heard strange hoots and noises from the forest around them, everyone was soon shivering.
3. After the first storyteller finished, another camper began a tale, and it was scarier.
4. In this story, a boy who didn't believe in ghosts agreed to stay in a haunted house overnight, and his friends couldn't talk him out of it.
5. After he had been in the house for an hour or so, he began to hear strange noises, but they didn't frighten him.
6. The camper who told the story added sound effects, for he knew how strange sounds scare people.
7. When he came to the "Boo!" at the end of the story, half of the campers jumped and screamed, and the rest laughed in relief.

B. Identifying Kinds of Sentences

Identify each sentence below with **S** for simple, **CD** for compound, **CX** for complex, or **CD-CX** for compound-complex.

1. The governor chose the best people whom he could find for the committee; Mr. Dobbs was appointed committee chairman. ______
2. The shopping mall has a store that sells nothing but clocks. ______
3. The most valuable of the prizes was wrapped in tattered and dirty paper. ______
4. People who expect special treatment are often disappointed. ______
5. Kathy had planned to study for the test this morning, but she overslept. ______
6. What we learned about France made us eager to visit that country, but we don't save money quickly, so the trip will not come soon. ______
7. The family planned outdoor activities for every day of vacation; however, bad weather interfered with the plans. ______
8. Every summer my cousins and uncle go to the opening baseball game. ______

Name _______________________________________ Date _______________

Lesson 5

Compound-Complex Sentences

Application

A. Identifying Kinds of Sentences

Identify each sentence in the short ghost story below with **S** for simple, **CD** for compound, **CX** for complex, or **CD-CX** for compound-complex.

1. One evening, George was driving in thick fog, and he took a shortcut past the cemetery. _______

2. When he saw a young woman walking slowly along in the dark, he pulled over to offer her a ride. _______

3. A cold, damp wind came into the car with the young woman. _______

4. The hitchhiker rode silently until the car reached the boundary of the cemetery, and there she disappeared. _______

B. Writing Different Kinds of Sentences

Write compound-complex sentences by adding to the sentences in Exercise A according to the directions in parentheses.

1. (Locate the compound sentence in Exercise A. Add an adjective clause.)

____

____

2. (Locate the complex sentence in Exercise A. Add another independent clause that gives more detail about the young woman's response.)

____

____

3. (Locate the simple sentence in Exercise A. Add a complex sentence—independent clause plus an adjective, adverb, or noun clause—that tells George's reaction to the coldness.)

____

____

4. (Locate the compound-complex sentence in Exercise A. Replace either independent clause.)

____

____

CHAPTER 8

Name ______________________________ Date ______________

Lesson 1

Agreement in Number

Teaching

CHAPTER 9

A verb must agree with its subject in number. **Number** refers to whether a word is singular (naming one) or plural (naming more than one).

A singular subject takes a singular verb.

Jon enjoys adventure. (singular subject, singular verb)

A plural subject takes a plural verb.

Adventurous people enjoy travel. (plural subject, plural verb)

In a sentence with a verb phrase, the first helping verb must agree with the subject.

He has hiked the Grand Canyon, and they have gone white-water rafting.

The **contractions** *doesn't* and *don't* are short forms of *does not* and *do not.* Use *doesn't* with all singular subjects except *I* and *you.* Use *don't* with all plural subjects, *I,* and *you.*

Doesn't the Grand Canyon look beautiful?

Don't people ride donkeys or horses to the bottom of the Grand Canyon?

Making Subjects and Verbs Agree in Number

In each sentence, underline the subject. Then underline the verb in parentheses that agrees with the subject.

1. Volcanoes (erupts, erupt) in countries all over the world.
2. Some people (watches, watch) volcanoes.
3. They try to predict when a volcano (is, are) going to erupt.
4. The watchers (warns, warn) the people who live nearby.
5. The closest towns' residents (moves, move) to a safer area.
6. A volcano watcher (has, have) an opportunity to save lives.
7. In addition, watchers (gathers, gather) information for scientists.
8. This activity (is, are) very dangerous.
9. Some volcano watchers (is, are) killed at work.
10. A watcher (has, have) to be extremely careful.

B. Identifying Subjects and Verbs That Agree in Number

In each sentence, underline the subject and the verb. On the line following the sentence, write whether the two parts of the sentence **Agree** or **Disagree** in number.

1. Juggling are not easy. ______________
2. The activity require a lot of practice. ______________
3. The world's best jugglers throw as many as ten balls. ______________
4. Jugglers uses balls, hoops, or clubs. ______________
5. Many performers include juggling in their acts. ______________

Name ______________________________ Date ______________

Lesson 1

Agreement in Number

More Practice

CHAPTER 9

A. Making Subjects and Verbs Agree in Number

On the line following each sentence, write the present tense form of the verb that agrees with the subject.

1. Mountain climbing (be) a sport of climbing to the summit of mountains. ____________
2. People (climb) mountains for many reasons. ____________
3. Climbing (appeal) to many people's sense of adventure. ____________
4. Other people (be) attracted by the challenge of scaling difficult slopes. ____________
5. A climber (need) extensive training. ____________
6. A beginner (practice) on cliffs that are easier to climb. ____________
7. Mountain climbers (keep) themselves in top physical condition. ____________
8. A climber (learn) how to use specialized equipment. ____________
9. Most climbing accidents (happen) to people who lack training and experience. ____________
10. Otherwise, mountain climbing accidents (be) rare. ____________

B. Correcting Agreement Errors

In each sentence, underline the subject once and the verb twice. If the verb agrees with the subject, write **Correct** on the line to the right. If it does not agree, write the correct verb.

1. My mother bakes delicious apple pies. ____________
2. Tim's sunburn feel painful. ____________
3. The steak was as tough as shoe leather. ____________
4. The band members practices every day. ____________
5. In my garden, the first flowers has bloomed. ____________
6. Every year, my aunt sends me interesting gifts. ____________
7. I has never visited our state capital. ____________
8. We enjoys watching the sunset at the beach. ____________
9. Lisa and Heidi is co-editors of the school newspaper. ____________
10. A kangaroo carry its young in a pouch. ____________

Name ______________________ Date ______________

Lesson 1

Agreement in Number

Application

A. Proofreading for Errors in Agreement

Underline the five verbs in this paragraph that do not agree with their subjects. On the lines below, write the numbers of the sentences in which you find agreement errors. After each sentence number, write the subject and the verb form that agrees with it.

(1) Astronauts risk their lives working in space. **(2)** The word *astronaut* comes from the Greek language. **(3)** The Greek words means *sailor among the stars.* **(4)** Pilot astronauts command the spacecraft. **(5)** Mission specialists conducts experiments. **(6)** All astronauts has been trained for weightlessness. **(7)** They experiences the near absence of gravity on large airplanes. **(8)** For about 30 seconds, they float weightlessly as the plane climbs and dives. **(9)** All the astronauts is asked to prove their physical and mental fitness. **(10)** For everyone who becomes an astronaut, the training process is a long one.

____

____

____

____

____

____

B. Making Subjects and Verb Agree in Writing

Choose one of the topics below and write a paragraph of at least four sentences about it. Use the present tense throughout. Make sure the subjects and verbs of all the sentences agree.

____

____

____

____

____

____

____

____

A visit to a planetarium
Life on other planets
A trip to the moon
Using a telescope

Living on a space station
Walking in space
Being weightless
Why I want to be an astronaut

CHAPTER 9

Name ______________________ Date __________

Lesson 2

Compound Subjects

Teaching

CHAPTER 9

A **compound subject** is made up of two or more simple subjects joined by a conjunction such as *and, or,* or *nor.*

And A compound subject whose subjects are joined by *and* usually takes a plural verb.

> The radio **and** the CD player are both playing.

Sometimes a compound subject joined by *and* is used as a single unit and takes a singular verb.

> Macaroni and cheese is one of my favorite meals.

Or* or *Nor When the parts of a compound subject are joined by *or* or *nor,* the verb should agree with the part closest to it.

> **Neither** the speakers **nor** the music sounds clear.
>
> **Either** a new CD player **or** better speakers are needed.

Making Verbs Agree with Compound Subjects

In each sentence, underline each part of the compound subject. Underline twice the word joining the parts. Then underline the verb in parentheses that agrees with the subject.

1. The school's front door or side entrances (is, are) going to be open for tonight's orchestra program.
2. Neither the night buses nor the subway (go, goes) to the school.
3. My uncle or my grandparents (plan, plans) to drive me there on time.
4. The violin and cello (is, are) orchestra instruments.
5. Neither the violins nor my viola (was, were) in tune.
6. Strings and percussion (make, makes) an interesting combination.
7. Either Ms. Meade or her assistants (has, have) the programs.
8. The classroom clocks and my watch (disagrees, disagree).
9. Neither practice nor rehearsals (prepares, prepare) performers completely for a performance in front of an audience.
10. Either the music teachers or the principal (is, are) going to say something.
11. Musicians and parents (is, are) invited to a reception after the concert.
12. Either the first song or the last two pieces (is, are) my personal favorites.
13. Neither the musicians nor the conductor (is, are) tired yet.
14. The parents and relatives (are, is) applauding loudest.
15. Either the trumpeters or the tuba player (leaves, leave) the stage last.
16. Students and teachers (is, are) already anticipating next year's concert.

Name ______________________________ Date ______________

Lesson 2

Compound Subjects

More Practice

A. Making Verbs Agree with Compound Subjects

In each sentence, underline each part of the compound subject. Underline twice the word joining the parts. Then underline the verb in parentheses that agrees with the subject.

1. Either the jugglers or the magician (perform, performs) next.
2. Neither the brownies nor the pie (taste, tastes) good.
3. The Baileys and Lees (is, are) neighbors.
4. Either the early Greeks or mythology (is, are) a good topic for your research paper.
5. Neither scary movies nor the dark (frighten, frightens) me.
6. Both the Scouts and their leader (know, knows) the way to the campsite.
7. Neither the bread nor the bananas (is, are) on sale this week.
8. Both the index and the glossary (is, are) in the back of the book.
9. The librarian or the science teachers (help, helps) me find books for my project.
10. Neither my brothers nor my father (like, likes) mushroom pizza.

CHAPTER 9

B. Using the Correct Verb with a Compound Subject

Choose and write the correct form of the given verb.

1. Either some dogs or a raccoon (have, has) raided the garbage. ______________
2. Both ocean liners and lake vessels (dock, docks) here. ______________
3. Neither Illinois nor Indiana (have, has) mountain ranges. ______________
4. Neither the tent nor the sleeping bags (arrive, arrives) until later in the week. ______________
5. The orchestra and the band (are, is) playing together at the assembly. ______________
6. Either the coach or the co-captains (call, calls) time. ______________
7. Neither the players nor the coach (have, has) left the locker room yet. ______________
8. Both beagles and basset hounds (howl, howls) a lot. ______________
9. Either the first violinist or the teacher (play, plays) that part. ______________
10. Neither the crew members nor the pilot (were, was) injured. ______________

Name ________________________________ Date ______________

Lesson 2

Compound Subjects

Application

CHAPTER 9

A. Correcting Errors in Agreement

Find the mistakes in the paragraph. For each sentence, write the correct present tense verb to agree with the compound subject. If the verb does agree, write **Correct.**

(1) Several students and our music teacher is forming a new jazz band. **(2)** Neither the students nor Mr. Blaine has much time for practice. **(3)** But for us, neither orchestra music nor band tunes is totally satisfying. **(4)** Our trumpeter and the drummer has played in jazz bands before. **(5)** Either Mr. Blaine or the two experienced jazz players has selected the other members of the group.

1. ______________________________

2. ______________________________

3. ______________________________

4. ______________________________

5. ______________________________

B. Using the Correct Verb with Compound Subjects

Write a sentence using each compound subject given and a verb in the present tense. Add words to the given subject as needed for the sense of the sentence.

1. The conductor and the musicians ______________________________

____

2. Either the newspaper or the television announcers ______________________________

____

3. Neither the ice nor the snowdrifts ______________________________

____

4. A parrot or a turtle ______________________________

____

5. The players and their coach ______________________________

____

6. Neither the school bus nor the teachers' cars ______________________________

____

Name ______________________________ Date ______________

Lesson 3

Agreement Problems in Sentences

Teaching

Subjects in Unusual Positions In some sentences, unusual word order makes the subject hard to find. When a sentence is the form of a question, begins with a phrase, or begins with *here* or *there,* reorder the words, putting the subject before the verb to decide whether the verb should be singular or plural.

Question:	Is that book interesting?
	That book is interesting.
Here and There:	Here are the new magazines.
	The new magazines are here.
Beginning phrase:	In the library are meeting rooms.
	Meeting rooms are in the library.

CHAPTER 9

Predicate Nouns A predicate noun follows a linking verb and describes the subject. The verb must agree with the subject, not the predicate noun.

My favorite reading material is **mysteries.**
Mysteries are my favorite reading **material.**

Prepositional Phrases The subject of a verb is never part of a prepositional phrase. Mentally block out any words between the subject and verb. Make the verb agree with the subject.

Books about baseball entertain fans. (plural subject and verb)

Baseball on the field or in books entertains fans. (singular subject and verb)

Making Subjects and Verbs Agree

Underline the subject of each sentence. Then underline the verb that agrees with the subject.

1. Here (is, are) the latest issue of the newsletter.
2. One pleasant result of the production number (was, were) demands for encores.
3. The cause of most earthquakes (is, are) the release of stress along a fault.
4. There (was, were) several clowns in the little car.
5. In the line (stand, stands) the patient ticket buyers.
6. Assignments from that teacher (is, are) always challenging.
7. (Is, Are) the children's petting zoo nearby?
8. The program about great moments in the 1990s (repeat, repeats) tonight.
9. Many hearing problems (is, are) a product of constant, loud noise.
10. There (is, are) two letters for you.
11. (Do, Does) that dog have a collar and tag?
12. The list of names of winners (is, are) being read now.
13. Into the pool (jump, jumps) the hot children.
14. Where (is, are) your new puppy?

Name ______________________________ Date ______________

Lesson 3

Agreement Problems in Sentences

More Practice

A. Making Subjects and Verbs Agree

Underline the subject. Then underline the verb that agrees with the subject.

1. The edges of the playing field (was, were) rimmed with ice.
2. The nurses at Dr. Stone's office always (seems, seem) pleasant.
3. There (wasn't, weren't) enough dictionaries for the whole class.
4. (Does, Do) voices sound different on a tape recording?
5. Here (is, are) the diamonds that our baseball teams always use.
6. From this potion (rises, rise) strange vapors.
7. Where (is, are) the boxes of cereal in this store?
8. All the nations along this line (pays, pay) close attention to seismologists' reports.
9. Why (doesn't, don't) Leslie join the group at the campground?
10. Under the bed (hides, hide) my timid kittens.

B. Correcting Agreement in Number

In each of these sentences, decide whether the verb agrees with the subject. If it does, write **Correct** on the line. If it does not, write the correct form of the verb on the line.

1. Were that baby-sitter willing to take care of four children? ______________
2. There was left-overs from the faculty luncheon. ______________
3. Here is the box of paper clips you need. ______________
4. Antique cars like the Model A costs thousands of dollars. ______________
5. Don't Uncle Matt write interesting letters? ______________
6. Where is the Seven Wonders of the World? ______________
7. Into the swamp slide the crocodiles. ______________
8. The number of accidents on this road have been increasing. ______________
9. Do the newspaper list all the cable stations? ______________
10. There is not enough volunteers at the shelter. ______________
11. The artwork on the gallery walls are priceless. ______________
12. Here is the cause of our problems. ______________

Name ______________________________ Date ______________

Lesson 3

Agreement Problems in Sentences

Application

A. Correcting Agreement in Number

Underline the subject and verb of each numbered sentence. If there is an agreement error, write the subject and the correct form of the verb on the lines below. If the subject and verb agree, write **Correct.**

(1) In our attic lies numerous old treasures. **(2)** One box of chipped dishes are not worth much in cash. **(3)** However, the worth of that box is the memories it holds for my mother. **(4)** Shelves at one end of the attic holds all our old dolls and games. **(5)** Don't everyone want to save souvenirs of all kinds?

CHAPTER 9

1. ______________________________

2. ______________________________

3. ______________________________

4. ______________________________

5. ______________________________

B. Making Subjects and Verbs Agree

In each sentence beginning below, underline the word that should be used as the simple subject in a sentence. Then supply a complete predicate, including a verb of your choice, to complete the sentence. Make sure your verb agrees with the underlined subject.

Example The waves on the shore *wash away our footprints.*

1. A band without trumpet players

____

2. The captain of the basketball team

____

3. The stores at the intersection

____

4. That ship beyond the rocks

____

5. The members of the crew

____

Name ______________________________ Date ______________

Lesson 4 Indefinite Pronouns as Subjects

Teaching

CHAPTER 9

An **indefinite pronoun** does not refer to a definite, or specific, person, place, thing, or idea.

When used as subjects, some indefinite pronouns are always singular. Others are always plural. Others can be singular or plural depending on how they are used.

Indefinite Pronouns					
Always Singular	another	each	everything	nothing	something
	anybody	either	neither	one	
	anyone	everybody	nobody	somebody	
	anything	everyone	no one	someone	
Always Plural	both	few	many	several	
Singular or Plural	all	any	most	none	some

Singular indefinite pronouns take singular verbs.

Each of the phones was ringing.

Plural indefinite pronouns take plural verbs.

A few of the calls were wrong numbers.

All, any, most, none, and *some* can be singular or plural. If the pronoun refers to a single person or thing, it takes a singular verb. If it refers to more than one person or thing, it takes a plural verb.

Most of these **dates** are correct. (The *dates* are considered as individuals.)

Most of the **information** is correct. (*Information* is considered as one quantity.)

Making Indefinite Pronouns and Verbs Agree

In each item, underline the indefinite pronoun used as the subject. If the pronoun changes number according to the noun it refers to, also underline that noun. Then find the verb. If the verb agrees with the subject, write **Correct.** If not, write the correct verb form.

Example None of the callers was ready to sign up. *were*

1. None of the students is absent. ______________
2. Each of the parents send care packages during the two weeks. ______________
3. Nobody is going into the water in this high wind. ______________
4. Some of the milk have turned sour. ______________
5. Both of the twins go to summer camp. ______________
6. Everyone wants to be a winner. ______________
7. Most of the team members get a team picture. ______________
8. Someone were supposed to bring the net. ______________
9. Several of the girls has made the all-star team. ______________
10. Most of the children has brought lunches. ______________

Name ______________________________ Date ______________

Lesson 4

Indefinite Pronouns as Subjects

More Practice

A. Making Verbs Agree with Indefinite Pronoun Subjects

In each sentence, underline the indefinite pronoun used as subject. If the pronoun changes number according to the noun it refers to, underline that noun. Then find the verb. If the verb agrees with the subject, write **Correct.** If not, write the correct verb form.

1. Several of the campers has arrived early. ______________

2. Most of the neighbors was away on vacation. ______________

3. Someone are dropping off campers in the parking lot now. ______________

4. Somebody was trying to leave a message. ______________

5. Was any of Brianna's classmates going to camp? ______________

6. One of the girls have become ill. ______________

7. Nobody like to be left out. ______________

8. A few of the counselors has brought snacks. ______________

9. Both of my best friends were unable to attend. ______________

10. Several of Josh's friends is enrolled in computer camps. ______________

B. Using Verbs with Indefinite Pronoun Subjects

Write each numbered sentence on the appropriate line, using the correct present tense form of the verb.

(1) Most of this troop's members (want) to become Eagle Scouts in a few years. **(2)** Some of the boys (plan) ahead. For example, Jacob keeps track of all the badges he needs to earn. **(3)** Some of the work he does for his badges (be) helpful in his studies. **(4)** All of his free time (be) devoted to his service project. **(5)** None of his relatives (have) ever become Eagle Scouts.

1. ____

2. ____

3. ____

4. ____

5. ____

CHAPTER 9

Name ______________________________ Date ______________

Lesson 4

Indefinite Pronouns as Subjects

Application

CHAPTER 9

A. Checking Agreement of Verbs with Indefinite-Pronoun Subjects

Proofread this paragraph for errors in subject-verb agreement. Underline any verb that does not agree with the indefinite pronoun used as its subject. On the lines below, write the number of each sentence that has an error and rewrite the sentence correctly.

Jonathan's main summer activity is soccer camp. **(1)** Most of the boys and girls of Jonathan's age is in the advanced group. **(2)** Some of the motivation for the boys is to be better than the girls. **(3)** In fact, one of the girls are better than all of the boys. **(4)** Everybody play 20 minutes of every 40-minute game. **(5)** Several of the camp participants disagree with this policy. **(6)** However, none of the responses from the coaches suggest the policy will change.

____

____

____

____

____

____

B. Using Verbs Correctly with Indefinite Pronouns as Subjects

In each sentence beginning below, underline the word that should be used as the simple subject in a sentence. Then supply a complete predicate, including a present-tense verb of your choice. Make sure your verb agrees with the underlined subject.

Example Some of the certificates *have not been signed.*

1. Most of the day

2. All of the soccer players

3. None of the pizza

4. Both of the goalies

5. Everyone in the stands

6. One of the coaches

7. Each of the parents

8. Most of the ceremony

Name ______________________ Date ______________

Lesson 5

Problem Subjects

Teaching

CHAPTER 9

The following guidelines can help you decide whether the subject in a sentence is singular or plural.

Collective Nouns A collective noun names a group of people or things. Examples include *group, team, family, class,* and *majority.* When the members act together, the collective noun takes a singular verb. When they act as individuals, it takes a plural verb.

Next week, the club publishes its final report to the school. (acting together)

The club are completing their research projects. (acting as individuals)

Nouns Plural in Form Some nouns ending in *–s* or *-ics* appear to be plural but are considered singular. As subjects, these nouns take singular verbs. Examples include *news, measles, mathematics, mumps, civics, physics, acoustics,* and *molasses.*

Mathematics has many fields of study, including geometry and algebra.

Titles Titles of works of art, literature, or music are singular.

The Frogs is a play usually presented in swimming pools.

Measures and Amounts Words and phrases that identify weights, measures, numbers, and time are usually considered singular. Fractions are considered singular or plural depending on whether the subject is thought of as a whole or as separate objects.

Two ounces of the spice costs more than I want to spend. (singular)

Four hours is required for developing the film. (singular)

Only two-fifths of the packages have been delivered. (plural)

Using Verbs That Agree with Problem Subjects

In each sentence, underline the subject and the form of the verb that agrees with it.

1. The lacrosse team (has, have) won the championship.
2. The parents' committee (has, have) been unable to agree on award winners.
3. *The Fantasticks* (is, are) the play that the drama club is performing.
4. Three dollars (are, is) the price of a raffle ticket.
5. A majority (have, has) voted for Benjamin, who is now the school president.
6. The honors club (is, are) offering free tutoring to the students.
7. Five inches of snow (are, is) enough for the school to close for the day.
8. Acoustics (are, is) the study of sound.
9. "Four days (are, is) plenty of warning for a test," replied the teacher.
10. Two-thirds of the students (is, are) part of an athletic team.
11. Thirty dollars (is, are) the price for the team sweatshirt.
12. "Two-fourths of any amount (equal, equals) one-half of it," answered the student.
13. The art class (meets, meet) only once a week.
14. *Around the World in 80 Days* (is, are) the book that the literature class is reading.
15. Economics (is, are) not a popular class for many high school students.

Name ______________________________ Date ______________

Lesson 5

Problem Subjects

More Practice

CHAPTER 9

A. Using Verbs That Agree with Problem Subjects

In each sentence, underline the verb that agrees in number with the subject.

1. One-half of the students (are, is) participating in extracurricular activities.
2. Physics (is, are) offered only to high school juniors and seniors.
3. Three dollars (has, have) for years been the price for a school lunch.
4. The soccer team (practices, practice) every other day.
5. *The Planets* (are, is) the first work on today's orchestra program.
6. The group (argue, argues) about extending the school day.
7. Six years (was, were) a long time to wait for a championship title.
8. Three-fourths of our time (was, were) spent in choosing a name for the yearbook.
9. Athletics (is, are) an important part of the extracurricular activities at the school.
10. The troop (meet, meets) every Tuesday night to discuss upcoming events.

B. Correcting Subject-Verb Agreement

If the verb agrees with its subject, write **Correct** on the line. If it disagrees, write the correct form of the verb.

1. The war news were not good. ______________
2. The hard-working staff deserves their days off. ______________
3. *Circular Forms* was painted by Robert Delaunay. ______________
4. The jury has delivered its opinion. ______________
5. Slightly over 26 miles are run by every successful marathon runner. ______________
6. Economics deals with the production and use of goods and services. ______________
7. Two-thirds of the milk were spoiled by morning. ______________
8. One-half of the marbles have fallen off the table. ______________
9. The class have voted unanimously for Cheryl. ______________
10. "We Three Kings" are a traditional holiday carol. ______________

Name ______________________________ Date ______________

Lesson 5

Problem Subjects

Application

A. Proofreading for Subject-Verb Agreement

Proofread this paragraph for errors in subject-verb agreement. Draw a line through each incorrect verb. Then draw this proofreading symbol ⌃ next to the word and write the correction above the error.

The school orchestra are holding a performance this week at the local music center. Five dollars are the price of the tickets for students, and seven dollars are the price for nonstudents. We are hoping that a large audience turn out for the show. The orchestra is performing a variety of songs. *The Pines of Rome* are to be played, for example. The audience are going to be encouraged to sing along with popular songs on the program. Two-thirds of the profit from the performance are to be spent on new sheet music.

B. Writing Sentences

Complete each of these sentences by adding a verb in the present or present progressive tense that agrees with the subject and any other needed words.

Example Three-fourths of the pudding *has been eaten already*.

1. The debate club ______________________________

____

2. Two-fifths of these magazines ______________________________

____

3. "The Three Little Pigs" ______________________________

____

4. Six pounds ______________________________

____

5. Mathematics ______________________________

____

Name ____________________ Date ____________

Lesson 1

People and Cultures

Teaching

CHAPTER 10

Follow these rules of capitalization:

- Capitalize people's names and initials.

  Lyndon B. Johnson   Ulysses S. Grant

- Capitalize titles and the abbreviations of titles used before names or in direct address. Capitalize the abbreviations of some titles when they follow a name.

  Colonel Blake   Dr. Jane Elway   Hello, Professor   Luis Hernandez, M.D.

- Capitalize titles of heads of state, royalty, or nobility only when they are used with a person's name or in place of a person's name. Do not capitalize titles when they are used without a proper name.

  Sir Walter Raleigh   The Prince of Wales visited the United States.

  The queen wore a crown.

- Capitalize the titles indicating family relationships only when the titles are used as names or parts of names. Do not capitalize a family name when it follows the person's name or is used without a proper name.

  Aunt Vicky   Grandma Ellen   My uncle   Ellen, our aunt.

- Always capitalize the pronoun *I*.
- Capitalize the names of religions, sacred days, sacred writings, and deities. Do not capitalize the words *god* or *goddess* when they refer to a group of dieties, as in ancient mythology.

  Christianity   Kwanza   the Book of Genesis   Allah

- Capitalize the names of nationalities, languages, races, and some ethnic groups, and the adjectives formed from these names.

  the French   Portuguese   Caucasian   Polish   German sausage

Capitalizing Names of People and Cultures

Underline the words that should be capitalized in each of the following sentences.

1. My sister and I love thai food.
2. Can I have another piece of that delicious french bread?
3. This book is about aztec pyramids.
4. The hindu god shiva is the patron of dancers.
5. In 1979, prime minister margaret thatcher was elected.
6. According to a greek myth, the god zeus was the father of hercules.
7. The new professor at the college is dr. jeffrey a. long
8. For his bar mitzvah, my cousin joel memorized a passage from the torah.
9. The duke of marlborough was an ancestor of sir winston churchill.
10. When grandpa joe comes to visit, he tells us stories about when he was in the army with colonel jack s. anderson.

Name ______________________________ Date ______________

Lesson 1

People and Cultures

More Practice

A. Capitalizing Names

Underline the letters that should be capitals in each of the following sentences. If the sentence is already correct, write **Correct.**

1. We read a short story by e. b. white. ____________

2. The opening address was given by senator nancy holland. ____________

3. Can ms. nold arrange an appointment with rev. thomas? ____________

4. My new french teacher is canadian. ____________

5. The principal invited capt. williams to speak at the assembly. ____________

6. My father and uncle henry both enjoy books written by martin prescott, ph.d. ____________

7. My brother and I saw grandpa victor downtown. ____________

8. Several times a day, muslims pray to allah. ____________

9. Ask mom if dad is ready to pack the camper. ____________

10. In norse mythology, the god odin is ruler over the other gods, and his son is thor. ____________

11. Romans often gave new names to the gods of greek mythology. ____________

12. In greek mythology, the god of war was named ares; in roman mythology, the god of war's name was mars. ____________

CHAPTER 10

B. Capitalizing Correctly

Underline each word that should be capitalized in the following paragraph. Not every sentence has a word that need to be capitalized.

(1) John jay was an early american statesman. **(2)** He was the president of the Continental Congress from December 1778 until September 1779. **(3)** He then became the american ambassador to Spain. **(4)** He was acquainted with general george washington. **(5)** In 1789, president george washington appointed jay the first chief justice of the Supreme Court. **(6)** In 1794, chief justice jay traveled to England and negotiated a treaty with the english government. **(7)** He resigned as chief justice when he was elected governor john jay of New York. **(8)** As a diplomat, patriot, and chief justice, john jay played an important role in early american history.

Name ______________________________ Date ______________

Lesson 1 People and Cultures

Application

A. Proofreading

Proofread the following first draft of a report. Look especially for errors in capitalization. Draw three lines under each letter that should be capitalized.

EXAMPLE William howard taft was an american politician.

Many young people dream of being the president of the United States. Instead, william howard taft wanted to be a justice of the U.S. Supreme Court. On the way to reaching his goal, taft served as the U.S. president from 1909 to 1913. During his presidency, admiral robert peary became the first person to reach the North Pole. The norwegian explorer roald amundsen led an expedition to the South Pole. The chinese republic was founded. The english ship *Titanic* sank in the Atlantic Ocean. Although these were exciting times, president taft was not happy. When he left the White House, he announced, "I'm glad to be going." Eight years later, president warren g. harding appointed taft chief justice of the Supreme Court. Chief justice taft considered this office to be a greater honor than being president of the United States.

B. Writing with Capital Letters

Suppose it was your job to introduce a panel of speakers to an audience. You would need to announce each speaker's name and tell a little about him or her. Write an introduction for an imaginary panel of four speakers. Be sure to capitalize all the names and titles correctly.

Name ______________________________ Date ______________

Lesson 2

First Words and Titles

Teaching

Capitalize these words:

- the first word of every sentence
- the first word of every line of traditional poetry
- the first word of a direct quotation if it is a complete sentence (Do not capitalize the first word of the second part of a divided quotation unless it starts a new sentence.)

  "My favorite book is *Where the Red Fern Grows,*" said Lesley.

  "We just bought," exclaimed Owen, "two tickets to see *The Miser* next week."
- the first word of each item in an outline and letters that introduce major subsections

  I. Types of literature

  A. Drama

  1. Comedy

  2. Tragedy
- the first word in the greeting of a letter and the first word in the closing
- the first word, the last word, and all other important words in titles (don't capitalize articles, conjunctions, or prepositions of fewer than five letters.)

CHAPTER 10

Capitalizing First Words and Titles

Underline the words that should be capitalized in each of the following items.

1. "i like," Luther commented, "reading a play before I go to see it."
2. each year, we read several plays in our English class.
3. this year we will read and then see a live performance of *macbeth* by William Shakespeare.
4. dear Lynette,

   The Festival Playhouse is pleased to announce that you have been selected to play Juliet in our upcoming performance of *romeo and juliet.* Congratulations.

   sincerely,

   Cleo Wilson, President, Festival Playhouse
5. Aisha said, "my favorite playwright is Tennessee Williams, who wrote *the glass menagerie.*"
6. "many plays," Mrs. Richardson explained, "have been turned into successful musicals, such as *pygmalion,* which is better known as *my fair lady.*"
7. I. drama

   a. elements of drama

   1. plot

   2. character

Name ______________________ Date ______________

Lesson 2

First Words and Titles

More Practice

A. Capitalizing First Words and Titles

In the following sentences underline the words that should be capitalized but are not. If the sentence contains no capitalization errors, write **Correct** on the line.

1. "Watch out!" warned the mine inspector. "the cable has snapped!" ____________

2. In *julius caesar,* Mark Antony says, "friends, Romans, countrymen, lend me your ears." ____________

3. "I think," said the doctor, "that you need a good rest." ____________

4. the sun that brief December day ____________

rose cheerless over hills of gray ____________

John Greenleaf Whittier ____________

5. we read the poem "a certain slant of light" by Emily Dickinson. ____________

6. natalie sang "the star-spangled banner" before the kickoff. ____________

7. ralph can play "down in the valley" and "the yellow rose of Texas" on the guitar. ____________

8. "did you hear," Ida asked, "our classmate Brian playing the piano at the talent show?" ____________

9. all students of American government should read *the federalist papers.* ____________

10. "many paintings," our art teacher told us, "are based on stories from Greek mythology, such as the story of Icarus and his wax wings." ____________

B. Capitalizing First Words in Outlines

Underline each letter that should be capitalized in the following outline.

Works of Edgar Allan Poe

I. poems

- **a.** "annabel lee"
- **b.** "the raven"

II. tales of horror

- **a.** "the pit and the pendulum"
- **b.** "the masque of the red death"
- **c.** "the fall of the house of usher"

CHAPTER 10

Name ______________________ Date ____________

Lesson 2

First Words and Titles

Application

A. Writing a Conversation

Continue the conversation of two people coming out of a theater. The speakers have seen an award-winning movie, but they have differing opinions about it. Have the two speakers compare this movie (you can decide which movie) with other movies they have seen. Include at least two other titles. Be sure to capitalize the quotations and titles correctly.

"I can see why that movie got the award," said Glenn. "It was one of the best movies I've ever seen."

"Well, I didn't think it was that good," replied Gina. "In fact, I can name at least two films I liked better. One of them should have gotten the award."

____

____

____

____

____

____

CHAPTER 10

B. Writing an Outline Using Capital Letters Correctly

Read the following brief report. Then write a short outline for it on the lines below. Be sure to capitalize correctly.

Laura Ingalls Wilder was born in Wisconsin in 1867. Her family moved around, and she grew up living on the American frontier. In 1885 she married farmer Almanzo Wilder. They survived through some hardships and eventually settled in Missouri.

Many years later, at the urgings of her daughter, Wilder began to write about her childhood. Her books became known as the Little House series, beginning with *Little House in the Big Woods.* The books, including *Little House on the Prairie* and *On the Banks of Plum Creek,* were loosely based on her family's westward travels. For her work she won five Newbery Medals and received the first Laura Ingalls Wilder Award.

The Life of Laura Ingalls Wilder

I. Early life

____

____

II. Later life

____

____

Name ______________________ Date ____________

Lesson 3 Places and Transportation

Teaching

Follow these rules of capitalization:

- In geographical names, capitalize each word except articles and prepositions. Geographical names include the names of continents *(Antarctica),* bodies of water *(Danube River),* islands *(Philippines),* mountains *(Ural Mountains),* other land forms *(Devil's Tower),* world regions *(Far East),* nations *(Russia),* states *(Georgia),* cities *(Atlanta),* and streets *(Peach Street).*
- Capitalize the names of planets and other specific objects in the universe. Do not capitalize *sun* and *moon* or *earth* when it is preceded by *the.*

  Mercury   Andromeda Galaxy   Halley's Comet
- Capitalize the words *north, south, east,* and *west* when they name particular regions of the country or world, or when they are parts of proper names. Do not capitalize words that indicate general directions or locations.

  South Carolina   The bus turned west on Main Avenue.
- Capitalize the names of specific buildings, bridges, monuments, and other landmarks.

  Statue of Liberty   Grand Central Station
- Capitalize the names of specific airplanes, trains, ships, cars, and spacecraft.

  Maine   *Challenger*

CHAPTER 10

Capitalizing Names and Places

Underline the words that should be capitalized in each of the following sentences. If the item is capitalized correctly, write **Correct** on the line.

1. If space travel were possible, I would surely visit mars. ____________
2. The taj mahal in india must be a wondrous sight. ____________
3. When we went to boston, massachusetts, last month, I enjoyed seeing the *u.s.s. constitution.* ____________
4. Can you name two countries in southeast asia? ____________
5. My grandmother has never left her home state, Texas. ____________
6. One continent no one in my family has visited yet is africa. ____________
7. The tower bridge in london crosses the thames river. ____________
8. Wouldn't it be exciting to walk along the great wall of china? ____________
9. Because the dead sea is so salty, it is easy to float in it. ____________
10. If you travel west from st. louis, you will eventually reach the rocky mountains. ____________

Name ______________________ Date ____________

Lesson 3

Places and Transportation

More Practice

A. Recognizing Words That Need Capitalization

Underline the words that should be capitalized in each of the following sentences. If the item is capitalized correctly, write **Correct** on the line.

1. When visiting san francisco, don't miss golden gate park. ____________

2. The mormon trail began in nauvoo, illinois, and ended in salt lake city. ____________

3. Will the northwest tollway take us to lake geneva? ____________

4. As we headed southeast, we saw the western edge of the alleghenies. ____________

5. Charles Lindbergh flew the *spirit of st. louis* across the atlantic ocean to paris. ____________

6. Explorer David Livingstone named victoria falls, which is on the zambezi river. ____________

7. On the west side of the Capitol is the National Mall. ____________

8. Napoleon Bonaparte was exiled to saint helena, a small island in the south atlantic ocean. ____________

B. Capitalizing Names of Places

Write the words that should be capitalized in each sentence.

1. Lewis and Clark explored the louisiana territory, traveling west from st. louis.

____

2. The statue of liberty was a present given to the united states by france.

____

3. The second largest city in russia is st. petersburg, which is located by the gulf of finland.

____

4. In B.C. 239, the appearance of halley's comet was recorded in china.

____

5. In florida, I'd like to see cape canaveral, where the *freedom 7* spacecraft was launched.

____

6. Before the fall of the berlin wall, berlin was divided into east berlin and west berlin.

____

CHAPTER 10

Name ______________________________ Date ______________

Lesson 3

Places and Transportation

Application

CHAPTER 10

A. Capitalizing Names of Places

Underline the words that should be capitalized in the following paragraph.

Come with me to new orleans. This exciting city is located in the southeast corner of louisiana on the mississippi river. It was founded by the French in 1718 and was named for a regent of france. Probably the most well-known area of the city is the french quarter. In the center of the french quarter is jackson square, where you can see a statue of Andrew Jackson on horseback. Jackson defended new orleans during the War of 1812. jackson square is surrounded by the saint louis cathedral and two former government buildings, the cabildo and the presbytière. The french market, a building with many shops, is east of the square on decatur street. The ursuline convent, thought to be the oldest building in the mississippi valley, stands on nearby chartres street. Many people flock to bourbon street to hear jazz and see its famous French and Spanish architecture.

B. Using Capital Letters in Writing

Write a paragraph about a vacation or trip you have gone on or would like to go on. In a short paragraph, name and describe at least four places—natural features, states, bodies of water, streets, or landmarks—that you saw or would like to see on your trip. Be sure to capitalize their names correctly.

Name ______________________________ Date ______________

Lesson 4 Organizations and Other Subjects

Teaching

Use capital letters for the following:

- all important words in names of organizations, institutions, stores, and companies

  Franklin Historical Association   Danville Middle School

- the abbreviations of organizations, businesses, and institutions by using the initial letters of the complete name (Notice that these abbreviations do not usually take periods.)

  ASPCA (American Society for the Prevention of Cruelty to Animals)

- names of historical events, periods, and documents

  Spanish-American War   Middle Ages   U.S. Constitution

- the abbreviations B.C., A.D., A.M. and P.M.
- names of months, days, and holidays but not the names of seasons except when used as part of a festival or celebration

  Tuesday, May 5   Memorial Day   Fall Concert

- names of school subjects only when they refer to language courses, when the subject is followed by a course number, or when it contains a proper adjective (Capitalize the word f*reshman, sophomore, junior,* or *senior* when it is used as a proper noun.)

  English Chemistry II   Senior Awards Ceremony

- names of special events and awards

  Pumpkin Festival   Pulitzer Prize

- brand names of products but not a common noun that follows a brand name

  Sleepytime slippers

Identifying Correct Capitalization

Underline the words or letters that should be capitalized in each of the following sentences.

1. The lee high school senior class is preparing a time capsule to be buried on new year's day.
2. The winter festival celebration is being organized by the senior class council.
3. The time capsule burial will be sponsored by super grocer's mart.
4. The history class is donating a newspaper about the end of the cold war.
5. The french class suggests adding an audio tape with their voices recorded on it.
6. Should we add items related to radio or TV, such as articles about npr or the bbc?
7. Maybe we'll add popular products such as flower shampoo and chocofun cereal.
8. One freshman will be selected to sing the lee high's school song when the ceremony begins on january 1 at 9:30 a.m.
9. Perhaps the time capsule will stay buried until 3000 a.d. or later.

CHAPTER 10

Name ______________________________ Date ______________

Lesson 4

Organizations and Other Subjects

More Practice

A. Capitalizing Names of Organizations and Other Subjects

Underline each letter that should be capitalized in the following sentences.

1. The battle of waterloo was fought on june 18, 1815.
2. The spring concert will take place on april 16.
3. My sister will enroll at the university of california at davis in the fall.
4. Volunteers from the variety club gave presents to the children.
5. During the middle ages, plagues caused many deaths.
6. Doctor Paglia performs surgery at northwestern memorial hospital.
7. Don't forget to buy me a wonder marker to use for my poster display.
8. The first ten amendments to the constitution are called the bill of rights.
9. Do you know when the treaty of versailles was signed?
10. I hope to be placed in the honors english class and algebra 2 next year.

CHAPTER 10

B. Capitalizing Correctly

Rewrite every sentence that contains a capitalization error. If a sentence is capitalized correctly, write **Correct** on the line.

1. The actress on this television show deserves an award for her work.

   ____

2. somerville plastics company is known as spc.

   ____

3. Representatives of 50 nations met in 1945 to draft the united nations charter.

   ____

4. My grandparents flew to Florida on sunshine airlines.

   ____

5. The senior class will choose five seniors to receive special awards.

   ____

6. For halloween, my art class always enters the Midville pumpkin decorating contest.

   ____

7. Mount Vesuvius erupted in a.d. 79, completely burying a thriving city.

   ____

Name ______________________________ Date ______________

Lesson 4

Organizations and Other Subjects

Application

A. Proofreading for Capitalization Errors

Jackson Middle School has been working on creating a time capsule. For the past few weeks, students and faculty have been suggesting what to include in it. Read the following speech given at the final ceremony before they bury the capsule. Draw three lines under any letters that should be capitalized but are not.

EXAMPLE Welcome to this year's time capsule burial ceremony.

Jackson middle school is thrilled to see so many people here this memorial day. Our school has worked tirelessly with students, faculty, and the sga to choose the items to go into our capsule. The capsule now contains current newspapers, CDs, and photographs of the school, as well as the popular shannon's trading cards and litestep shoes. We heartily thank the fine folks at shane's place for donating some current clothing items, namely jeans, sneakers, and dresses, to be included in the capsule. We have also included the essay written by the winner of the jackson literature award, Shania Byfield. Shania wrote her predictions for the world in a.d. 2100, when the capsule will be opened. Okay, digmaster construction company, start the digging!

B. Using Capitalization in Writing

Write sentences that combine names from any two categories listed below. First tell the categories you have chosen. Then write your sentence.

organizations	institutions	stores	companies	historical events
historical periods	documents	days	months	holidays
events	awards	brand names	time abbreviations	

EXAMPLE I am combining *documents and historical periods.*
The treaty of Versailles ended World War I.

1. I am combining ______________ and ______________.

   Sentence: ______________________________

2. I am combining ______________ and ______________.

   Sentence: ______________________________

3. I am combining ______________ and ______________.

   Sentence: ______________________________

4. I am combining ______________ and ______________.

   Sentence: ______________________________

5. I am combining ______________ and ______________.

   Sentence: ______________________________

CHAPTER 10

Name ________________________________ Date ______________

Lesson 1 Periods and Other End Marks *Teaching*

The three end marks are the period, question mark, and exclamation point. They are used to indicate the end of a sentence.

Periods Use a period at the end of a **declarative sentence.** A declarative sentence makes a statement.

Last year we vacationed in Wisconsin.

Use a period at the end of almost every **imperative sentence.** An imperative sentence gives a command. If a command expresses excitement or emotion, it ends with an exclamation point.

Tell me about your trip. Don't leave out a thing!

Use a period at the end of an **indirect question.** An indirect question reports what a person asked without using the person's exact words.

Thomas asked what happened.

CHAPTER 11

Use a period after an **abbreviation** or an **initial,** as in this example: Mr. Nelson R. Diaz.

Use a period after each number and letter in an **outline** or **list.**

Question marks Use a question mark to end an **interrogative sentence,** or question.

Where did you go in Wisconsin?

Exclamation points Use an exclamation point to end an **exclamatory sentence,** that is, a sentence that expresses strong feeling. Use an exclamation point after an **interjection** that expresses strong emotions.

No kidding! I don't know where to begin!

Using Periods and Other End Marks

Add punctuation as necessary in the following items.

1. Have you ever been in the Midwest

2. My mother grew up on a farm

3. She said there were more cows than people in her county

4. What a learning experience farm life must have been

5. My father, on the other hand, is from Washington, DC

6. Good grief I can't imagine what they found in common

7. The Midwest has always been a major food supplier to the rest of the nation

8. I Cereal crops

A Wheat (focus on Minn, Neb, SD)

B Corn (focus on Wisc, Ia, Ill, Ind)

II Meat products

A Beef

B Pork

Name ______________________________ Date ______________

Lesson 1

Periods and Other End Marks

More Practice

A. Using End Marks

Add punctuation marks where necessary in the following items.

1. My mother asked me if I had ever seen an egret before
2. It was right there in front of me Beautiful
3. What else did you see on your walk
4. Ice fishing is a popular winter activity in Wisconsin
5. Dr Harmon said he liked to get out around 6 AM
6. I asked if I could go fishing sometime
7. Can you come back in the winter
8. Was F Scott Fitzgerald from Wisconsin
9. I wonder who settled Wisconsin
10. Tell me about the Swedes
11. I Wisconsin geography
    A Agricultural lands
    B The Dells
    C Forest lands
    D Lakes and rivers
    II Wisconsin history
12. Look There are bears in those bushes

B. Using End Marks in Writing

Add the correct end mark at the end of each sentence in the following paragraph.

The Midwest is an important region in economic terms__ But how does it rank as a vacationland__ We went to Wisconsin to visit relatives__ I didn't expect to see much more than the relatives themselves__ How wrong I was__ We spent some time in the Dells__ Wow__ What a ride we had on the river__ Baraboo gave me another surprise__ Who would expect circus history there__ We saw the zoo at Milwaukee, historic sites around the state, and the most peaceful scenery you could imagine__ I can't remember being bored during the whole two weeks we were there__ For me, that's unusual__ I'm not saying I want to go there every year__ How many people go back to any place two years in a row__ But ask me again in a couple of years if I'd like to visit Wisconsin__ Then set a date__

Name ______________________ Date ______________

Lesson 1

Periods and Other End Marks

Application

A. Using End Marks in Writing

Add periods, question marks, and exclamation points where necessary in the following paragraph. To add a period, insert this symbol ⊙. To add a question mark or an exclamation point, use a caret ^ and write the correct punctuation mark above it.

I've never been a bird-watcher I've never understood people who go out and do it as an organized activity. What's the point At least, that's how I used to feel But on my vacation last summer in Wisconsin, I took an early-morning walk one day In the half-light of dawn, in the mist along the Fox River, I saw an egret And it saw me We stood and looked at each other, and it seemed to accept me as part of the scene, nothing to fear Incredible The experience changed my attitude toward bird watching Now I go out whenever I can, hoping to run into an egret again

CHAPTER 11

B. Using End Marks in an Outline

Write an outline for a brief composition on a vacation you have taken, or one you would like to take, somewhere within the United States. List at least three things you plan to see (or saw) on the vacation. Then list three difficulties or possible problems that you would prepare for, such as unpredictable weather. Be sure to punctuate correctly.

Title:

I Things to see

A ______________

B ______________

C ______________

II Difficulties to prepare for

A ______________

B ______________

C ______________

Name ______________________________ Date ______________

Lesson 2

Commas in Sentences

Teaching

Commas are used to separate parts of a sentence.

Use a comma before the conjunction that joins the two independent clauses of a compound sentence. Do not use a comma to separate parts of a compound predicate.

> The capital of Canada is Ottawa, but Montreal is Canada's biggest city.

In a series of three or more items, use a comma after every item except the last one.

> Some of Canada's provinces are Quebec, Ontario, and British Columbia.

Use commas between two or more adjectives of equal rank that modify the same noun. The adjectives are of equal rank if you can substitute the word *and* for the comma.

> Canada and the U.S. have a peaceful, cooperative relationship.

Use a comma after an introductory word or phrase.

> Before the end of our trip, we took a group picture in front of Niagara Falls.

Use commas to set off one or more words that interrupt the flow of thought in a sentence.

> Most of Canada's population, I might point out, lives close to the United States.

Use commas to set off nouns of direct address.

> Jill, tell the border guard that all of us are American citizens.

Use commas to set off appositives that add extra information but are not needed to make the meaning of the sentence clear.

> The biggest city, Montreal, is the largest French speaking city outside France.

Use a comma whenever the reader might otherwise be confused.

> Before autumn, leaves start turning colors in the cool Canadian air.

CHAPTER 11

Using Commas Correctly

Insert commas where necessary in the following sentences.

1. The Saint Lawrence Seaway a major waterway allows ocean-going vessels to travel between the Great Lakes and the Atlantic Ocean.
2. At the end of construction in 1959 the Seaway had seven locks and a depth of at least 27 feet.
3. Roland what can you tell me about the Saint Lawrence Seaway?
4. From Montreal to Lake Ontario the Saint Lawrence is about 183 miles long.
5. The Lachine section I believe has an 18-mile canal and two locks.
6. Three of the five sections are located entirely in Canada and the other two sections contain segments in northern New York.
7. The Seaway provides a deep stable waterway for commercial ships.
8. The cargo shipments are largely wheat corn barley soybeans and iron.
9. After ice forms the Seaway closes for the winter months.

Name Live Pirrotti Date 10/16/12

Lesson 2

Commas in Sentences

More Practice

A. Using Commas

Insert commas where necessary in the following sentences.

1. The U.S.-Canada boundary in fact is about 4,000 miles long.
2. It winds from a fishing village in Passamaquoddy Bay Maine to Vancouver Island.
3. Did you know ~~LaTisha~~ Tozer that Americans account for about 80% of Canada's tourists?
4. We waited in a long line to go through customs on our way to Canada but we had almost no wait at all when we came back home.
5. The customs officer was a serious stern woman.
6. Unlike the United States Canada is a federal parliamentary democracy.
7. After we entered Canada we changed our speedometer to kilometers.
8. Washington Montana North Dakota and Minnesota are U.S. states that share long borders with Canada.
9. When the border appears the cars traveling to Canada must go through customs.
10. People living near the Canadian border naturally must go through customs often.

I ♡ CANA

CHAPTER 11

B. Proofread for Commas

Insert commas where they are needed. Use the proofreading symbol ,^.

Niagara Falls as you may know is on the Niagara River in western New York and southeast Ontario. It actually has two waterfalls. The Horseshoe Falls on the Canadian side is 176 feet high and the American Falls on the U.S. side is 182 feet high. Carrying about nine times more water than the American Falls the Horseshoe Falls has a crescent shaped crest line. An island Goat Island in New York separates the two falls. A small beautiful section of the American Falls near Goat Island is called Bridal Veil Falls. Since its formation 12,000 years ago erosion has pushed Niagara Falls upstream about seven miles.

Name ______________________ Date ____________

Lesson 2

Commas in Sentences

Application

A. Proofreading for Commas

Add commas there they are needed in the following paragraph. Use the proofreading symbol ^,.

Dora we will be visiting Glacier National Park in Montana. It's located as you know near the Canadian border. Glacier National Park borders the Waterton Lakes National Park in Alberta Canada and together they form the Waterton-Glacier International Peace Park. Named for glaciers the park still has about fifty active ones. The biggest glacier in the park Blackfoot Glacier is located on the northern slope of Blackfoot Mountain. The glaciers provide water to more than 250 lakes. The beautiful peaceful Lake McDonald is surrounded by tall cliffs. In the summer around 1,000 species of wildflowers grow in the park. Wild animals such as bears elks mountain lions eagles and bobcats roam the lands.

CHAPTER 11

B. Using Commas in Writing

Rewrite the sentences by following the directions in parentheses.

1. We packed before we left for Canada. (Include a series of items.)

   We packed ~~clothes such as~~ hats, shoes, Shirts, jeans, & jackets before we left for Canada.

2. Campobello Island is an island in Passamaquoddy Bay. (Include two adjectives of equal rank that modify the same noun.)

   Campobello Island is an isolated, small island in Passamaquoddy Bay.

3. We drove straight to Niagara Falls. (Include an introductory phrase.)

   After picking up Tazer in Toronto, Canada, we drove straight to Niagara Falls.

4. We saw our favorite animal at the national park. (Include a nonessential appositive.)

   ____

Name ______________________________ Date ______________

Lesson 3 Commas: Dates, Addresses, and Letters *Teaching*

Commas in dates Use a comma between the day of the month and the year. If the sentence continues, use a comma after the year also.

On December 25, 1776, Washington crossed the Delaware.

Commas in addresses Use a comma between the name of a city or town and the name of the state or country. If the sentence continues, use a comma after the name of the state or country.

What happened at Lexington, Massachusetts, in 1775?

Commas in letters Use a comma after the greeting of a friendly letter and after the closing of a friendly or business letter.

Dear Dad, Your daughter,

CHAPTER 11

A. Using Commas Correctly in Dates and Addresses

Insert commas where necessary in the following sentences.

1. The Revolutionary War started at Lexington and Concord Massachusetts.
2. The British surrender was at Yorktown Virginia on October 17 1781.
3. The Battle of Bunker Hill was actually fought on Breed's Hill in Charlestown Massachusetts.
4. The young Marquis Lafayette was with Washington at Valley Forge Pennsylvania.
5. On July 4 1837 the Concord battle monument was dedicated.
6. Do you suppose that on July 4 2037 there will be an anniversary ceremony there?

B. Using Commas Correctly in Dates, Addresses, and Letters

Insert commas where necessary in the following letter.

476 Crescent Avenue
Middleport NY 14006
April 10 2000

Dear Grandpa Jim

Since you are interested in American history, I want to tell you about our field trip this year to Fort Ticonderoga near Albany New York. The trip was fun, and I learned all about the Green Mountain Boys and their leader, Ethan Allen. On May 10 1775 the Vermont patriots took Fort Ticonderoga from the British in a surprise attack. The fort is a museum now. During a demonstration, the museum guide let me help fire a cannon!

Your loving granddaughter
Susan

Name ______________________________ Date ____________

Lesson 3

Commas: Dates, Addresses, and Letters *More Practice*

A. Using Commas Correctly in Dates and Addresses

Insert commas where necessary in the following sentences.

1. On December 16 1773 colonists of Boston Massachusetts objected to British taxes on tea by dumping a shipment of tea into the harbor.
2. Soon many were predicting war; on March 23 1775 Patrick Henry gave a speech in Williamsburg Virginia in which he said, "Give me liberty or give me death!"
3. Just a month later, on April 19 1775 the first battle of the Revolution was fought.
4. Shortly after, on June 15 1775 the Second Continental Congress, meeting at Philadelphia Pennsylvania, named George Washington head of the army.
5. Washington won an important battle at Trenton New Jersey on December 26 1776.
6. After the end of the war, the last British soldiers boarded ships to leave New York New York on November 25 1783.

CHAPTER 11

B. Using the Comma in Letters

Write these parts in the correct order on the lines below. Use commas where they are needed.

4700 Crescent Avenue Grandpa Jim Baltimore MD 21218	With love Dear Susan April 21 2000	It's been years since I've traveled through Albany New York and seen historic sites in the area. How were you lucky enough to be invited to take part in the cannon demonstration at Fort Ticonderoga? Did the cannon fire as it should?

____

____

____

____

____

____

____

Name ________________________________ Date ______________

Lesson 3

Commas: Dates, Addresses, and Letters

Application

A. Proofreading a Letter

Proofread the following letter for punctuation errors. Insert commas where necessary.

476 Crescent Avenue
Middleport NY 14006
May 6 2000

Dear Grandpa Jim

You asked about my class's field trip to Fort Ticonderoga and how I was chosen to help fire a cannon in the demonstration. During our tour of the fort, the guide asked us about events of the Revolutionary War. Here are two of his questions: What happened on July 4 1776? Who almost turned over the American fort at West Point New York to the British? Everyone in the class could answer the first question, but I was the only one who knew about Benedict Arnold. So the guide chose me to help him. By the way, the cannon made a noise, but it didn't shoot anything at all!

Your loving granddaughter
Susan

B. Writing with Commas

Imagine that you're a soldier in Washington's army at Valley Forge during the terrible winter of 1777-78, and you're writing a letter to a family member at home. On the lines below, write the letter. Use the form of a friendly letter, using commas correctly.

CHAPTER 11

Name ________________________________ Date ____________

Lesson 4

Punctuating Quotations

Teaching

A **direct quotation** is a speaker's exact words. Use quotation marks at the beginning and at the end of a direct quotation.

"Chicken pox is a contagious disease," the doctor said.

Use commas to set off the explanatory words used with a direct quotation, at the beginning, middle, or end of the quotation.

The doctor said, "Chicken pox is a contagious disease."
"Chicken pox," the doctor said, "is a contagious disease."

If the quotation itself is a question or exclamation, the question mark or exclamation point should be placed inside the end quotation marks. Commas and periods always go inside the end quotation marks.

"Wait**!**" Mom objected. "Did you remember to take your medicine**?**"

If the quotation is part of a question or exclamation, the question mark or exclamation point should be placed outside the end quotation marks.

Did the doctor say, "You need to have a booster shot"**?**

A **divided quotation** is a direct quotation that is divided into two parts by explanatory words. Both parts are enclosed in quotation marks. The first word in the second part is not capitalized unless it begins a sentence. Review the above examples to see how to punctuate and capitalize a divided quotation.

A **dialogue** is a conversation between two or more speakers. When writing dialogue, indicate a change in speaker by using a new paragraph and a new set of quotation marks.

"Mrs. Abdalla," the doctor asked, "how long have you had this cough?"
"Well, I have felt sick for over a week," Mrs. Abdalla replied.

An **indirect quotation** is a restatement, in somewhat different words, of what someone said. Do not use quotation marks to set off an indirect quotation.

The doctor told me that I should start feeling better soon.

CHAPTER 11

Using Quotation Marks

Add quotation marks where necessary in each of these sentences.

1. Angela asked, Did you hear that Julian has pneumonia?
2. Did she say, I was sick with the flu last weekend?
3. Ouch! the child wailed. That shot hurt!
4. Kyle, asked Quinn, was your ankle surgery a success?
5. I was hospitalized for bronchitis last year, said Adrian.
6. Oh! Kristen moaned. I don't feel well.
7. Dave had to leave school early yesterday, reported Joshua, because he felt sick.
8. Can you give me information about visiting hours? Megan asked the receptionist. Are there any age limits for visitors?

Name ______________________ Date ____________

Lesson 4

Punctuating Quotations

More Practice

A. Writing Sentences with Quotation Marks

Add quotation marks, commas, and end marks where necessary in each sentence. If the sentence is correct as is, circle the numeral before the sentence.

1. I can't wait to visit my cousin in the hospital next week said Monica.

2. The patient stated Dr. Saito has Lyme disease.

3. The doctor announced I plan to treat her infection with antibiotics.

4. Did Terryn say I'm having my tonsils removed next month?

5. Wait! cried Hector. Do I really need to have an operation?

6. Is a throat culture dangerous? asked Mike.
No the doctor said. It is a very common procedure.

7. Shaquille wants to know when his stitches will be removed.

8. Did the patient say Don't forget to sign my cast?

9. When will you feel well enough to come back to school asked Mr. Garvey.

10. Lindsey said I have to take my medicine every day because I have an ear infection.

CHAPTER 11

B. Using Quotation Marks

Add the necessary quotation marks to the dialogue below.

Did you hear? David said, Connie broke her leg yesterday in the soccer game.

How long will she have to be in a cast? asked Eric.

About six weeks, replied David. The doctor said it was a clean break and should heal quickly.

Jodie asked, Can we all sign her cast when she comes back to school tomorrow?

Sure, said David. Maybe we can have a cast-signing party. That should cheer her up!

Great! Eric said. Then when she gets it off, she can keep it and always remember our last soccer game!

Name ______________________ Date ____________

Lesson 4

Punctuating Quotations

Application

A. Correcting Misuse of Quotation Marks

Rewrite the following sentences, using quotation marks, commas, and end marks correctly.

1. Mindy said I'd like to go visit a friend who is in the hospital because of scarlet fever.

____

____

2. What is strep throat asked Caitlin. And how will Sasha get rid of it.

____

3. Lisa will most likely have a slow recovery, or so her doctor says explained Aida.

____

____

4. You have to get better soon, so we can go play basketball again stated Malcolm.

____

5. Did you hear the doctor say, Nicholas has the most unusual case of poison ivy I have ever seen.

____

____

B. Writing with Quotation Marks

Write a short dialogue that you might overhear in a hospital waiting room. Make sure that you indicate clearly who is speaking. Use quotation marks and other punctuation marks correctly.

____

____

____

____

____

____

____

____

CHAPTER 11

Name ______________________________ Date ______________

Lesson 5

Semicolons and Colons

Teaching

A semicolon separates elements of a sentence. It is stronger than a period, but not as strong as a comma.

Semicolons in Compound Sentences Use a semicolon to join the parts of a compound sentence if you don't use a coordinating conjunction.

> We discovered two sunken vessels; however, only one yielded pieces of gold.

Use a semicolon between the parts of a compound sentence if the clauses are long and complicated, or when one or more of them contain commas.

> Three ships sailed from Hispaniola; but only one, with a crew of 17 men, made it back to Spain.

Semicolons with Items in a Series When there are commas within parts of a series, use a semicolon to separate the parts.

> We tracked voyages from Cuba; Jamaica, south of Cuba; and Haiti, southeast of Cuba.

Colons Use a colon in the following ways: to introduce a list of items; after the formal greeting in a business letter; and between hours and minutes in expressions of time. When using the colon to introduce a list, use it only after nouns or pronouns.

> Dear Captain Phillips:
>
> We will arrive at 11:45 A.M. Dr. Johnson's talk will cover the following islands: Martinique, Trinidad, and Grenada.

Using Semicolons and Colons

Add semicolons and colons where they are needed in the following sentences. Replace or cross out commas if necessary.

1. Captain Kidd was tried and hanged, Sir Francis Drake was knighted by the queen.
2. In the 1500s and 1600s, pirate captains and navy commanders had common goals, and, to tell the truth, I don't see much difference between Kidd and Drake.
3. Thomas likes pirate stories, therefore, I recommended *Treasure Island.*
4. Alison likes three subjects language arts, history, and science.
5. We studied for three hours for that test, unfortunately, we studied the wrong material.
6. Let's ask Jonathan, he's the expert.
7. Sylvia is the most talented, however, she doesn't practice enough.
8. Successful diving for treasure depends on three things good research, good weather, and good luck.
9. The test is at 300, not 330.
10. This is a good treasure ground, but we didn't find anything valuable, except coral.
11. Treasure diving is fun, financing an expedition is hard work.
12. In the search of the ruins, one crew found gold, silver, and brass, but the other crew found wine bottles, wooden serving bowls, and an iron cooking pot.

Name ______________________ Date __________

Lesson 5

Semicolons and Colons

More Practice

A. Using Semicolons and Colons

Rewrite this book report, adding semicolons and colons where they are needed.

Treasure Island is one of the best pirate stories ever it's about an expedition in search of a buried treasure. It's written from the point of view of the good guys, but the most memorable character, without question, is a pirate, the one-legged Long John Silver. He has many attractive qualities great intelligence, leadership ability, and a fine sense of drama.

Another character, Ben Gunn, was once a pirate, however, the pirate crew to which he belonged left him marooned on Treasure Island. Now he joins forces with the good guys against Long John Silver and the pirates.

____

____

____

____

____

____

____

____

B. Using Semicolons and Colons

On the line to the right, write the word(s) from the sentence that should be followed by a semicolon or colon. Write the correct punctuation mark following each word. If the sentence is punctuated correctly, write **Correct.**

EXAMPLE Robert Louis Stevenson wrote these tales of adventure *Treasure Island, Kidnapped,* and *David Balfour.* adventure:

1. *Treasure Island* has all the elements of an exciting story intricate plot, interesting characters, dramatic situations, and suspense. ______________

2. It's full of suspense, but the good guys, some of whom are interesting, some of whom are dull, win out in the end. ______________

3. I stayed up until 10:30 three nights in a row reading it. ______________

4. Jim begins the treasure hunt, he finds a map in the trunk of an inn guest who dies. ______________

5. Jim gathers some trusted older friends to help him, but one of them, the squire, talks too much. ______________

CHAPTER 11

Name ______________________ Date ____________

Lesson 5

Semicolons and Colons

Application

A. Proofreading a Play Review

The critic who wrote this play review didn't know how to use semicolons and colons. Prepare her review for publication by adding the needed semicolons and colons.

The new play at the Phoenix is about a cartographer, a mapmaker, but it's more interesting than you might think. The cartographer is a mysterious man, almost from the start of the play you know he's hiding something. He lives in the early 1700s, and he's always searching for maps of the Caribbean, especially any islands visited by pirates. He never works with the maps, what is he looking for? The play has attractive qualities strong writing, humor, interesting characters, and a surprise ending, which I won't give away.

CHAPTER 11

B. Writing Sentences with Semicolons and Colons

For each item, write a sentence that matches the description in parentheses.

Example (sentence that uses a semicolon to join the parts of a compound sentence without a coordinating conjunction)
The treasure was hidden on an island; only one map showed its location.

1. (sentence that uses a colon in an expression of time)

____

2. (sentence that uses a semicolon to separate parts when commas appear within parts of a series)

____

3. (sentence that uses a semicolon to join the parts of a compound sentence without a coordinating conjunction)

____

4. (sentence that uses a colon to introduce a list of items)

____

Name ____ Date ______________

Lesson 6 Hyphens, Dashes, and Parentheses

Teaching

Here are ways to use the hyphen, the dash, and parentheses.

Hyphens Use a hyphen if part of a word must be carried over from one line to the next. Only words of two syllables or more may be broken, and at least two letters must be on each line. Make sure that the word is separated between syllables.

Correct:	val- ue	an- tique	old- er
Incorrect:	valu- e	ant- ique	o- lder

Use hyphens in certain compound words, such as *self-made* and *man-hour.*

Use hyphens in compound numbers from twenty-one through ninety-nine.

Use hyphens in spelled-out fractions, such as *one-sixth* and *two-eighths.*

Dashes Use dashes to show an abrupt break in thought.

Each model you see—don't touch!—requires weeks of work.

Parentheses Use parentheses to set off material that is loosely related to the rest of the sentence.

Making ships in bottles (which seems impossible) is an enjoyable hobby.

CHAPTER 11

A. Using Hyphens in Compound Words and Fractions

Write each of these words and phrases correctly, adding hyphens where needed.

1. fifty four stamps ______________________
2. two thirds complete ______________________
3. well balanced stamp collection ______________________
4. thirty two cent stamps ______________________
5. new self sealing stamps ______________________

B. Using Hyphens in Words Broken Between Lines

Underline each word that is broken correctly for use at the end of a line.

1. quart-er, dol-lar, nick-el, mone-y, bo-oks, penn-y
2. pict-ure, su- ccess, mod-el, bru-sh, eas-y, paint-ing

C. Using Dashes and Parentheses

Add dashes and parentheses where they are needed in these sentences.

1. My prized baseball card oh, no! is missing.
2. He has been making models airplanes are his favorite since he was a boy.
3. Putting together a model no matter how easy it may look always takes time.
4. Buying new baseball cards they are usually cheap is something I do quite often.
5. Shirley runs three miles every day it takes her half an hour.

Name ______________________ Date ____________

Lesson 6

Hyphens, Dashes, and Parentheses

More Practice

A. Using Hyphens in Compound Words and Fractions

Write each of these words and phrases correctly, adding hyphens where needed.

1. four fifths of the real size ____________
2. ill advised trading ____________
3. several half dollars ____________
4. eighty eight piano keys ____________
5. riding all of the merry go rounds ____________

B. Using Dashes and Parentheses

Add dashes and parentheses where they are needed in these sentences.

1. Reading mystery novels mostly the ones by Agatha Christie takes up my evenings.
2. Painting you should most definitely try it is a good way to express yourself.
3. She might if I have anything to say about it change her mind about selling her coins.
4. Horseback riding you must have guessed by now can be a dangerous sport.
5. The first stitch in needlework see the drawing below is an important one to learn.

CHAPTER 11

C. Using Hyphens, Dashes, and Parentheses Correctly

Rewrite each sentence, correcting punctuation errors. If a word at the end of a line is broken incorrectly, but there is a correct way of breaking it, show the word broken correctly in your revision. If the word may not be broken, move it to the second line.

1. Soccer (which is still more popular in
Europe has been my favorite pastim-
e since I was a young child.
2. When I play soccer as you probabl-
y already know—I play halfback.
3. Our team (which is called the Blaze-
rs) has been the division champion
for two years.
4. The playoff games you should com-
e to one—if you get the chance are
always very thrilling.
5. My coach says that if I keep practicing, I will make the varsity team.

Name ______________________ Date ____________

Lesson 6 Hyphens, Dashes, and Parentheses

Application

A. Proofreading for Correct Punctuation

Rewrite this paragraph on the lines below, adding or correcting the placement of hyphens, dashes, and parentheses as needed.

My brother as you might remember is a very talented juggler. Juggling which I find hard to learn—is the art of keeping two or more objects in the a-ir while tossing them back and forth in your hands. Four fifths of the time, he can juggle without dropping anything. He began as anyone would—with just three objects. Later, he wanted to try juggling, believe it or not, eggs! Howe-ver, we convinced him to try hard-boiled eggs first.

CHAPTER 11

B. Writing with Correct Punctuation

Follow the directions to write and punctuate sentences correctly.

1. Write a sentence that requires a hyphen.
2. Write a sentence that requires dashes and at least one hyphen.
3. Write a sentence that requires a hyphen and parentheses.
4. Write a sentence that requires two hyphens and either dashes or parentheses.

Name ______________________________ Date ______________

Lesson 7

Apostrophes

Teaching

Apostrophes are used in possessive nouns, contractions, and some plurals.

Apostrophes in possessives Use an apostrophe to form the possessive of any noun, whether singular or plural. For a singular noun, add *'s* even if the word ends in *s*.

Paul's ax   Jonas's lever

For plural nouns that end in s, add only an apostrophe.

the carpenters' tools   the workers' experience

For plural nouns that do not end in s, add an apostrophe and s.

the men's equipment   the deer's trails

Apostrophes in contractions A contraction joins two words by leaving some letters out. Use an apostrophes in a contraction to show where a letter or letters have been left out.

I would --> I'd   we will --> we'll   they have --> they've   she is --> she's

Don't confuse contractions with possessive nouns, which do not contain apostrophes.

it's (contraction, means *it is*)   its (possessive, means *belonging to it*)

Apostrophes in plurals Use an apostrophe plus *s* to form the plurals of letters, numbers, or words referred to as words.

Remember to cross your *t*'s.
When I began to read, I read *was*'s as *saw*'s.

Using Apostrophes

In each sentence below, underline the correct form of the two choices in parentheses.

1. The (levers / lever's) one of the simplest machines.
2. (Who's / Whose) able to name an even simpler one?
3. (Curtis's / Curtis') suggestion is the inclined plane.
4. He says (its / it's) simpler because there (arent / aren't) any moving parts.
5. Anna thinks (there / they're / their) using the term *machine* incorrectly.
6. "(What's / Whats') a machine?" she asks.
7. Her friends look up *machine* in (their / they're) dictionary.
8. (Its / It's) definition is "a device that performs work."
9. I guess (Im / I'm) confused about the (scientists' / scientists) definition of work.
10. While (your / you're) dictionary is open, look up *inclined plane.*
11. Look at that! There are four (*planes* / *plane's*) listed in the dictionary.
12. I think (we're / were) getting somewhere now.
13. (Let's / Lets) try to think of some other simple machines.
14. Is there anyone (whose / who's) willing to help me with this science unit?
15. These (children's / childrens / childrens') books on energy might be helpful.

Name ______________________ Date ______________

Lesson 7

Apostrophes

More Practice

A. Using Apostrophes Correctly

In each sentence below, underline the word that uses the apostrophe incorrectly or should have an apostrophe but does not. Then write the word correctly on the line.

1. The troopers cars have flashing red lights on the top. ____________
2. Theyre going to the store now for their supplies. ____________
3. The chorus has it's rehearsal on Tuesday nights. ____________
4. We're working through the list, but we're only up to the ms. ____________
5. She's sure its going to be all right with her mother. ____________
6. Charles' poem was selected for publication in his school's yearbook. ____________
7. The five student's parents will be guests of honor. ____________
8. Helens car wouldn't start, so she never made it to the game. ____________
9. Whos going to the graduates' dinner with you? ____________
10. Ive no idea who took your book. ____________

CHAPTER 11

B. Using Apostrophes in Possessives

On the lines below, rewrite all the underlined phrases in this paragraph, and replace them with phrases using possessives with apostrophes.

When I was young, I used to play in **(1)** <u>the workshop of my grandfather</u>, and watch him work. I was fascinated by **(2)** his <u>tools of the carpenter</u>. When I was older, I'd borrow **(3)** <u>the bike of my brother</u> and ride wherever new houses were being built. I'd stay out of **(4)** <u>the way of the men</u>, but I would try to get a close-up look at **(5)** <u>the equipment of the crew</u>. I knew I wanted carpentry to be **(6)** <u>the work of my life</u>. For years people kept telling me that construction wasn't **(7)** <u>the work of a woman</u>, but I didn't believe that. Finally **(8)** <u>the laws of the nation</u> supported my opinion. It took me a long time, but I finally got **(9)** <u>my card of a union member</u>. Now I'm eager to encourage **(10)** <u>the dreams of other girls</u> to do whatever work they like.

1. ______________________ 6. ______________________

2. ______________________ 7. ______________________

3. ______________________ 8. ______________________

4. ______________________ 9. ______________________

5. ______________________ 10. ______________________

Name ______________________________ Date ______________

Lesson 7

Apostrophes

Application

A. Proofreading for Use of the Apostrophe

Proofread the paragraph below for errors in the use of apostrophes. If a word uses an apostrophe incorrectly or is lacking a needed apostrophe, cross out the word. Then draw a caret ^ next to the error and write the word correctly above the error.

Have you ever thought of how a carpenters' tools find they're way into art and music? Think of a chisel, for example. It's operation depends on the principle of the inclined plane. Its a carpenter's machine. Yet its also a sculptors' machine. Without the hammer and chisel, they're would be no marble, granite, or wood statues. We would not have Michelangelos *David* or the Native Americans totem poles. The hammer and chisel have they're place in an orchestra, as well. Youll find the hammer in an orchestras' percussion section, and the chisel inside the woodwind's mouthpieces.

CHAPTER 11

B. Using Apostrophes in Writing

First rewrite each phrase below, using a possessive with an apostrophe. Then use your phrases in a paragraph about building a doghouse according to the directions in a magazine.

the dog of my family ______________________________

the size of the dog ______________________________

the directions of the writer ______________________________

the carpentry tools of my father ______________________________

the help of our neighbor ______________________________

Name ______________________________ Date ______________

Lesson 8 Punctuating Titles

Teaching

Quotation marks, italics, and underlining used correctly in titles show what kind of work or selection is named.

Quotation marks Use quotation marks to set off the titles of short works.

Quotation Marks for Titles			
Book chapter	"An Unexpected Party," from *The Hobbit*	**Magazine article**	"According to Herodotos"
Short story	"The Lottery"	**Song**	"Home on the Range"
Essay	"The American Scholar"	**Poem**	"Kubla Khan"

Italics and underlining Use italics for titles of longer works and for the names of ships, trains, spacecraft, and individual airplanes (but not the type of plane—Boeing 707). In handwriting, use underlining to indicate words that should be in italics in printed material.

Italics or Underlines for Titles			
Book	*Swiss Family Robinson*	**Epic poem**	*The Odyssey*
Play	*Macbeth*	**Painting**	*American Gothic*
Magazine	*Rolling Stone*	**Ship**	*U.S.S. Missouri*
Movie	*Beauty and the Beast*	**Train**	*Phoebe Snow*
TV series	*Law and Order*	**Airplane or Spacecraft**	*Apollo 11*
Long musical selection or CD	*Beethoven's Fifth Symphony*		

Punctuating Titles Correctly

Write each sentence, using quotation marks or underlining to set off titles.

1. The community theater group is putting on Shakespeare's A Midsummer Night's Dream.

   ____

2. The American Scholar is an essay by Ralph Waldo Emerson.

   ____

3. Apollo 11 was the spacecraft that took the first humans to the moon.

   ____

4. The Snows of Kilimanjaro is a short story by Ernest Hemingway.

   ____

5. The Sun Also Rises is one of Hemingway's best-known novels.

   ____

6. Anna sang Home on the Range, Red River Valley, and In the Gloaming for the pageant.

   ____

7. Calliope is a magazine for young people about world history.

   ____

CHAPTER 11

Name ______________________ Date ____________

Lesson 8

Punctuating Titles

More Practice

A. Punctuating Titles Correctly

In each sentence below, insert quotation marks where needed and underline words that should be italicized.

1. The Lusitania was torpedoed by a German U-boat; the Titanic struck an iceberg.
2. At Stratford, we saw productions of Macbeth, As You Like It, and Henry IV, Part I.
3. Sailing to Byzantium is one of William Butler Yeats's greatest poems.
4. The name of Charles Lindbergh's plane was Spirit of St. Louis.
5. Anne Morrow Lindbergh wrote a famous book entitled Gift from the Sea.
6. The Mariner 9 spacecraft orbited Mars; Mariner 10 flew by Venus and Mercury.
7. Do you know who wrote the music to The Star-Spangled Banner?
8. Ludwig van Beethoven's Ninth Symphony sets Friedrich Schiller's poem Ode to Joy to music.
9. I loved Lewis Carroll's Through the Looking-Glass and What Alice Found There, especially the chapter Humpty Dumpty.

CHAPTER 11

B. Punctuating Titles Correctly

Use each title given in parentheses in a sentence, punctuating the title correctly.

1. (play by Arthur Miller: The Crucible) ______________________

____

2. (short story by Nathaniel Hawthorne: Young Goodman Brown) ______________________

____

3. (magazine: Natural History) ______________________

____

4. (painting by Archibald Willard: The Spirit of '76) ______________________

____

5. (book by F. Scott Fitzgerald: The Great Gatsby) ______________________

____

6. (poem: Casey at the Bat) ______________________

____

Name ______________________________ Date ______________

Lesson 8

Punctuating Titles

Application

A. Punctuating Titles Correctly

Choose the person in your class that you think is least like you. Then, after filling out the column labeled "My favorites," interview the other person to discover his or her likes and dislikes. Remember to fill in the person's name at the top if the page. Use quotation marks and underlining to show italics.

	My favorite	____________'s favorite
Book		
Short Story		
Ship		
Movie		
Song		
CD		
Poem		
Play		

B. Punctuating Titles Correctly in Writing

Review the chart above. Then write a paragraph in which you identify which of the choices were easy and which were difficult. Mention some of the other works that you wanted to include in the chart. Or, if you have enough information from the classmate referred to in the chart, write the paragraph discussing his or her choices.

CHAPTER 11

Name ______________________ Date ____________

Sentence Parts

More Practice 1

Complete each diagram with the sentence provided.

A. Simple Subjects and Verbs

Athletes compete.

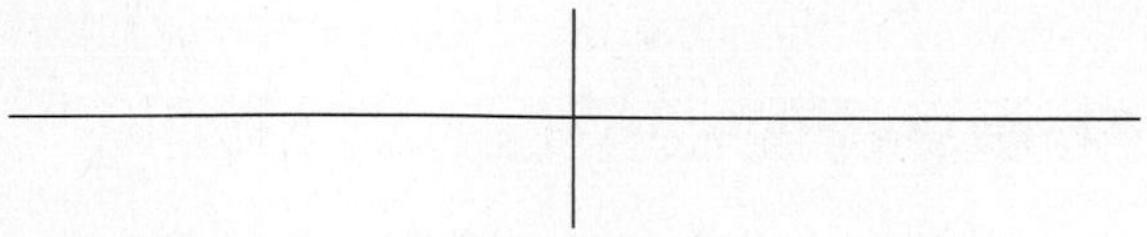

B. Compound Subjects and Verbs

Compound Subject Amateurs and professionals compete.

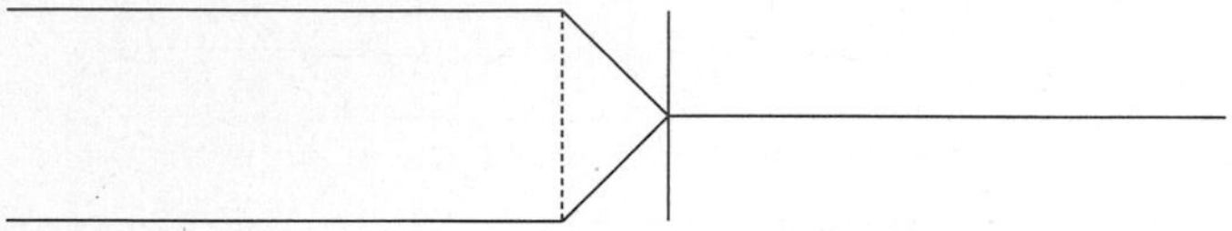

Compound Verb Athletes train and compete.

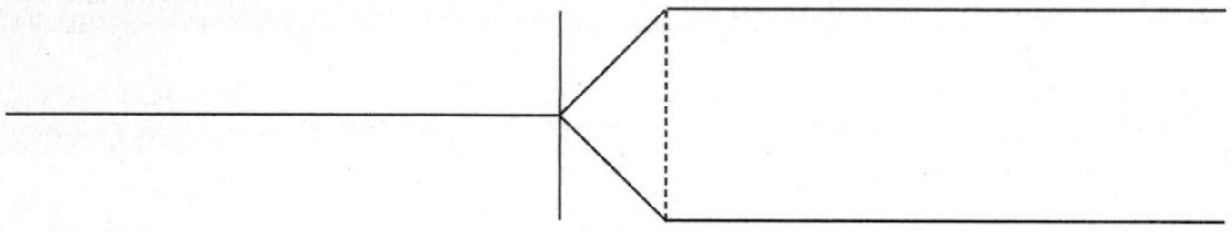

Compound Subject and Verb Amateurs and professionals train and compete.

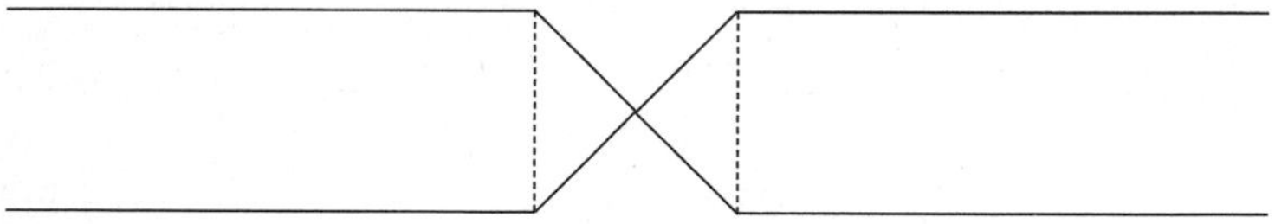

C. Adjectives and Adverbs

Adjectives and Adverbs The energetic sprinters are running very fast today.

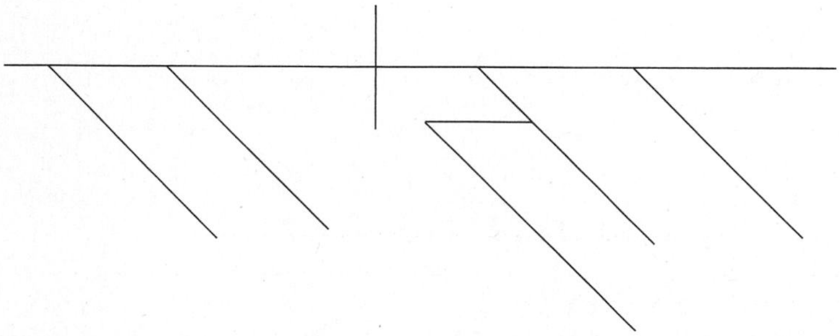

Name ______________________ Date ____________

Sentence Parts

More Practice 2

Complete each diagram with the sentence provided.

D. Subject Complements

Predicate Noun Jim Thorpe was an exceptional athlete.

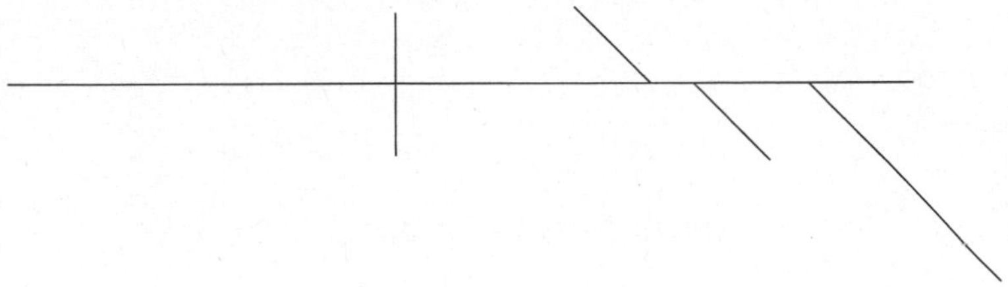

Predicate Adjective Thorpe seemed unbeatable.

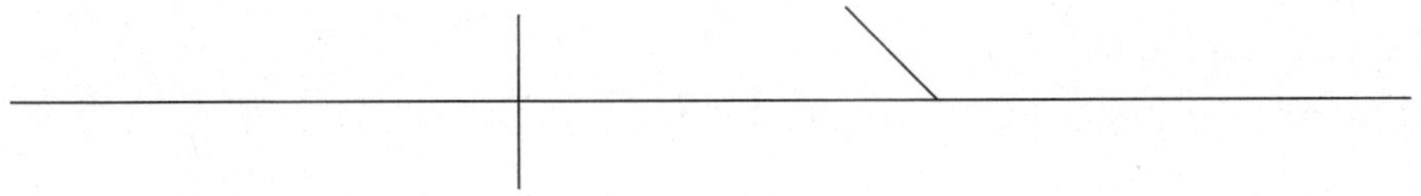

E. Direct Objects

Single Direct Object This outstanding athlete won Olympic medals.

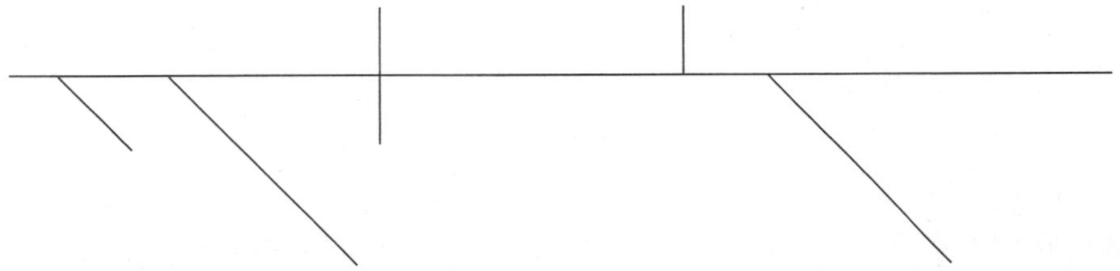

Compound Direct Object He played professional baseball and professional football.

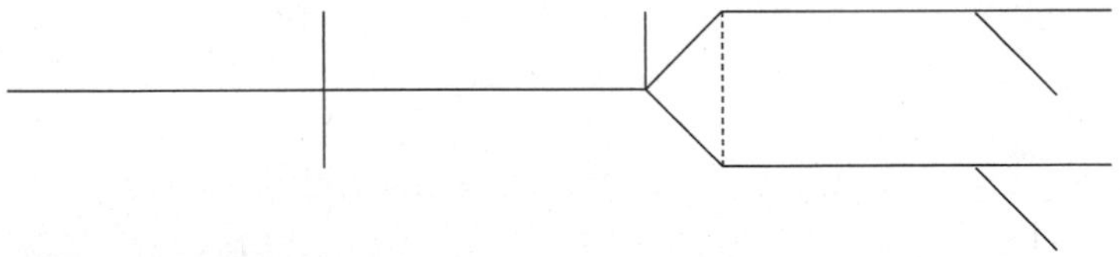

F. Indirect Objects

Thorpe brought his small school national fame.

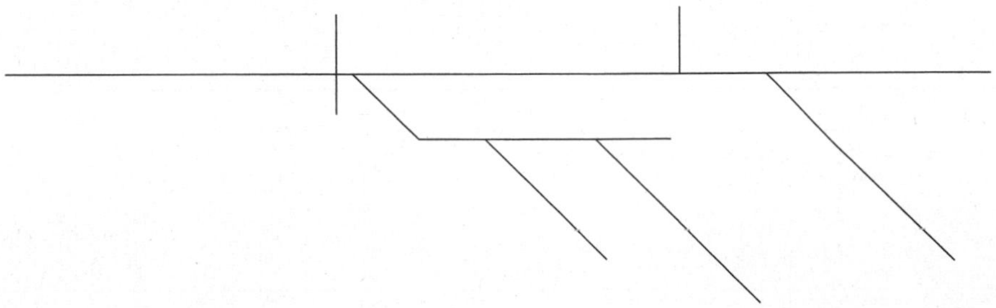

Name ______________________ Date ______________

Sentence Parts

Application

On a separate piece of paper, diagram each of these sentences.

A. Diagramming Subjects, Verbs, and Modifiers

1. Individuals and teams compete.
2. Some athletes excel.
3. The best players are not forgotten.
4. Fans watched and cheered.

B. Diagramming Subject Complements and Objects

1. Jim Thorpe was a Native American.
2. His career gave younger tribe members hope.
3. Football was just becoming popular.
4. Thorpe gave football fans thrills and memories.

C. Mixed Practice

1. Jim Thorpe won the 1912 pentathlon and decathlon.
2. The pentathlon and the decathlon are multi-event competitions.
3. The rules have changed.
4. The pentathlon is rarely held today.
5. The decathlon includes the long jump, the high jump, several races, and other events.
6. Judges award the best all-around athlete the medal.
7. Strong winds often give jumpers problems.
8. Thorpe's biography is an eventful one.

Name ______________________________ Date ______________

Phrases

More Practice 1

Complete each diagram with the sentence provided.

A. Prepositional Phrases

Adjective Phrases Storytellers of ancient times recited tales about the sun.

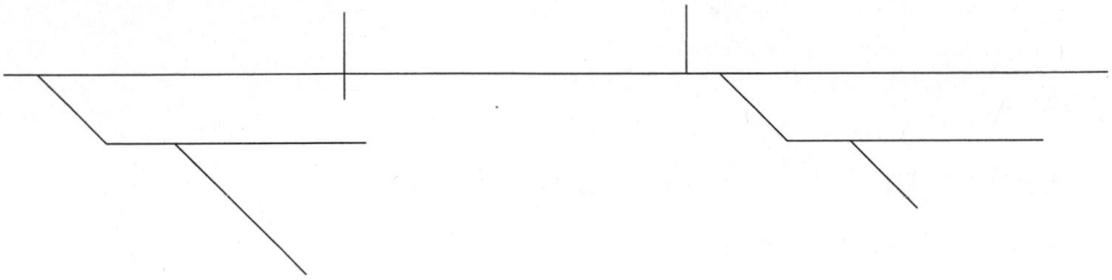

Adverb Phrases You have probably heard about several sun gods.

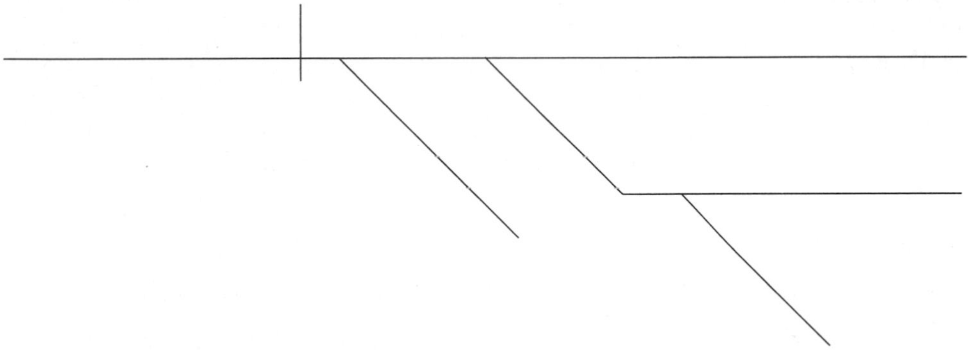

B. Participles and Participial Phrases

The surprising power of the sun still brings out amazed responses from humans.

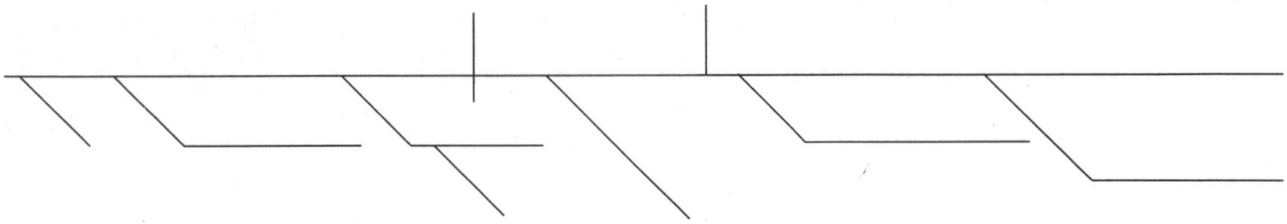

Light sent into space by the sun supports life on Earth.

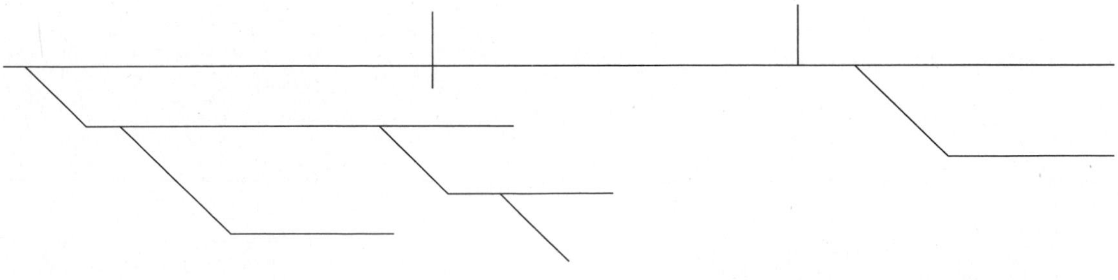

Name ________________________________ Date ________________

Phrases

More Practice 2

Complete each diagram with the sentence provided.

C. Gerunds and Gerund Phrases

Gerund Phrase as Subject Discovering facts about the sun requires careful observation.

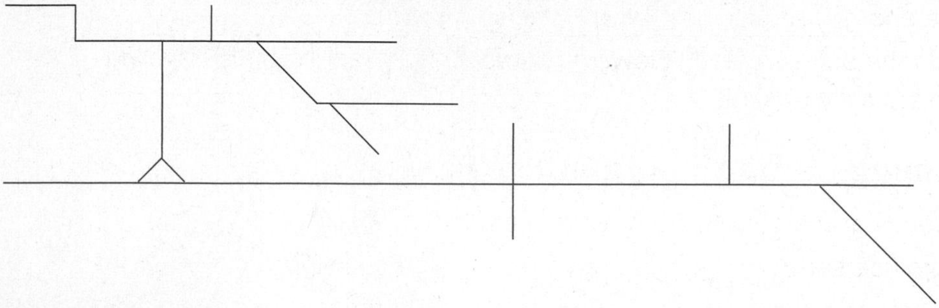

Gerund Phrase as Object of Preposition The sun's brightness interferes with observing this star.

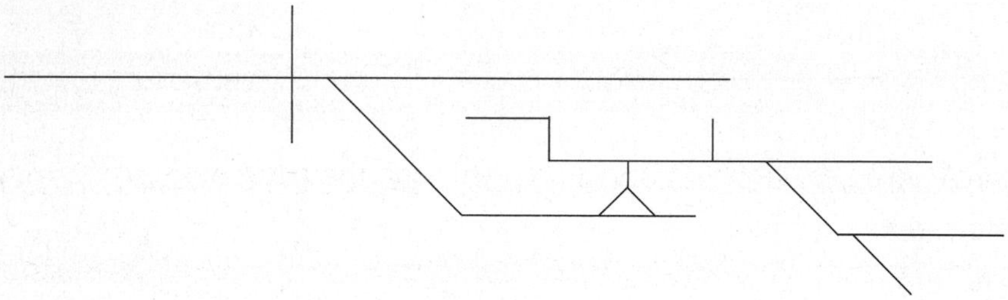

DIAGRAMMING

D. Infinitives and Infinitive Phrases

Infinitive Phrase as Noun Scientists want to learn about all stars through the sun.

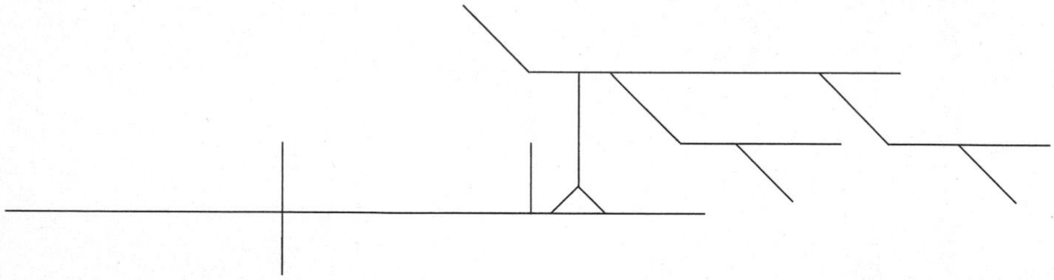

Infinitive Phrase as Modifier Astronomers have tried many ways to collect information about the sun.

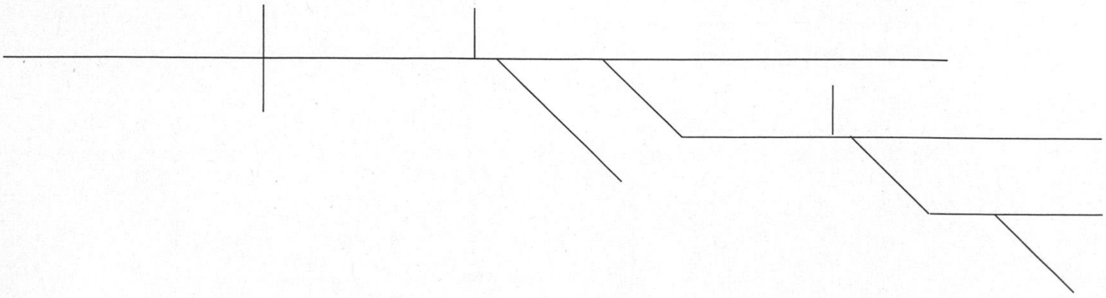

Name ______________________________ Date ______________

Phrases

Application

On a separate piece of paper, diagram each of these sentences.

A. Diagramming Prepositional and Participial Phrases

1. The sun is a star of medium size.
2. Spinning like a top, the sun moves through the Milky Way galaxy.
3. Most of the energy produced by the sun is lost in space.
4. Eruptions on the sun's surface, known as flares, disrupt radio signals traveling through Earth's atmosphere.

B. Diagramming Gerund and Infinitive Phrases

1. Looking directly at the sun will harm your eyes.
2. Astronomers use spectographs to analyze the colors in sunlight.
3. Studying these colors tells scientists about the sun's interior.
4. Other ways to learn about the sun include using radio telescopes.

C. Mixed Practice

1. To see the sun as a god came naturally to early civilizations.
2. To the Greeks, the sun was a shining god called Helios.
3. The Greeks imagined Helios driving his fiery chariot through the sky.
4. The Egyptians preferred to imagine the sun god in a boat.
5. Watching an eclipse terrified people in early days.
6. The sun, becoming dimmer by the minute, seemed to be dying.
7. Today, informed by astronomers, we are tempted to laugh at these fears.
8. The sun will continue to give us light for millenniums to come.

Name ______________________ Date ____________

Clauses

More Practice 1

Complete each diagram with the sentence provided.

A. Compound Sentences

Yellowstone National Park was created in 1872, and now the National Park System has 378 sites.

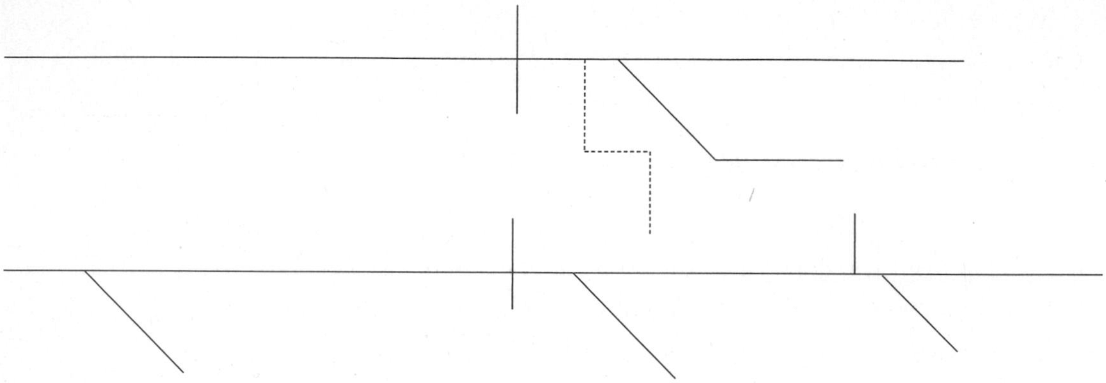

B. Complex Sentences

Adjective Clause

(Relative pronoun as subject) Yellowstone, which features steamy geysers, is a very popular destination.

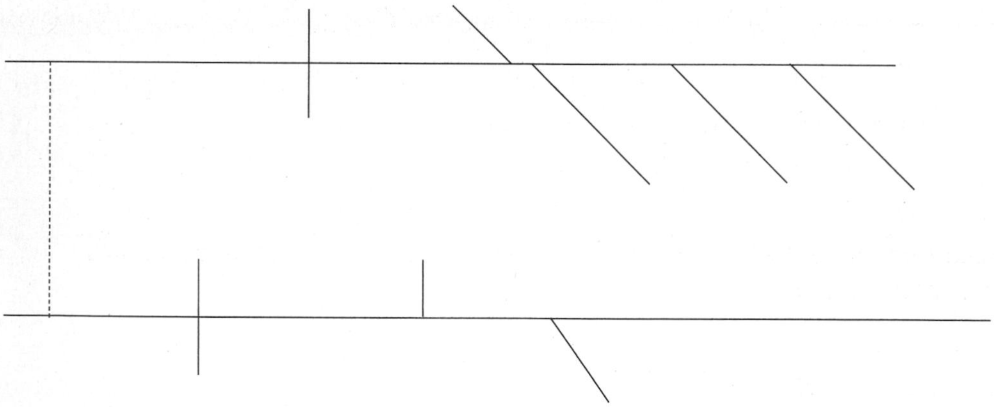

Adjective Clause

(Relative pronoun as object of preposition) We, for whom the parks were created, enjoy them in the summertime.

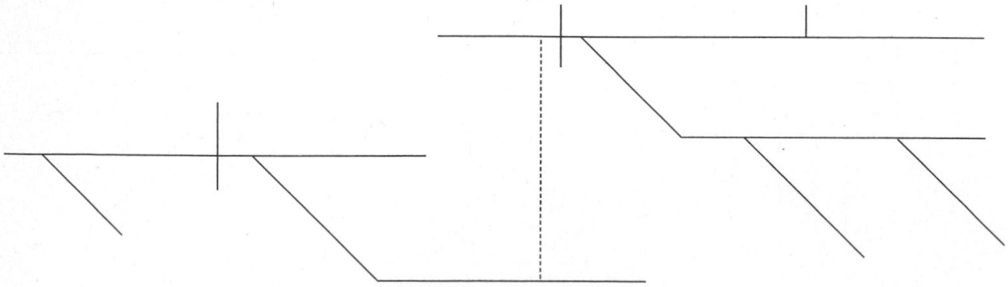

Name ______________________ Date ____________

Clauses

More Practice 2

Complete each diagram with the sentence provided.

B. Complex Sentences (continued)

Adverb Clause If you enjoy nature, consider visiting a site in the National Park System.

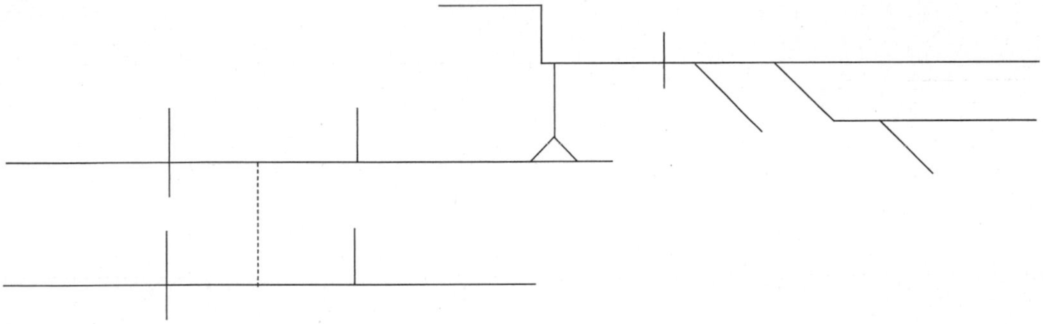

Noun Clause Used as Direct Object Many sites in the park system commemorate where historical events happened.

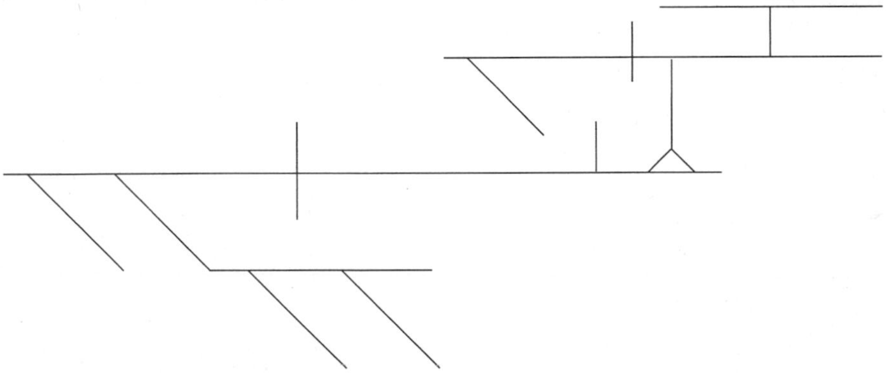

Noun Clause Used as Subject How our country developed is shown in memorials, monuments, and historic sites.

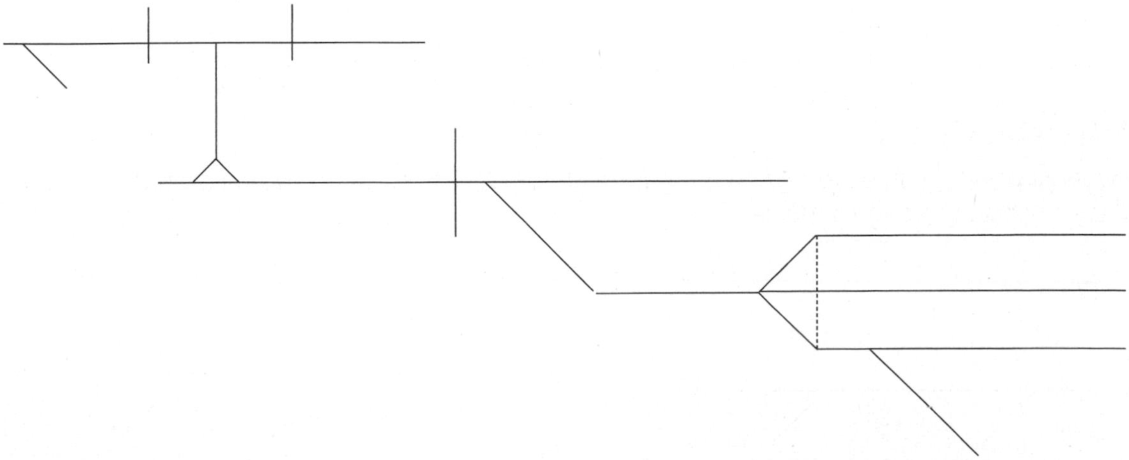

DIAGRAMMING

Name ______________________________ Date ______________

Clauses

Application

On a separate piece of paper, diagram each of these sentences.

A. Diagramming Compound Sentences and Complex Sentences (Adjective Clauses)

1. Millions of people visit the parks annually, and overcrowding has become a serious problem.
2. Gettysburg is a national military park that informs visitors about the Civil War.
3. One site that you might not recognize as a national parkland is the White House.
4. A park that draws people to Hawaii is the Volcanoes National Park, which has active volcanoes.

B. Diagramming Complex Sentences with Adverb and Noun Clauses

1. When night falls, visitors to Carlsbad Caverns National Park watch thousands of bats flying from Bat Cave.
2. How goldminers traveled to the Klondike is shown in the Klondike Gold Rush park.
3. If you walk across the National Mall in Washington, D.C., you are on Park System land.
4. Unless you live in Delaware, your state has at least one national parkland.

C. Mixed Practice

1. Most parklands are managed by the National Park Service, which is in the Department of the Interior.
2. Native Americans who lived in Colorado around 1000 A.D. occupied the cliff dwellings of Mesa Verde National Park.
3. Some parks offer visitors tram tours, or the visitors may hike on their own.
4. Before Columbus came to America, some trees in Sequoia National Park were already 2,000 years old!
5. Nobody who has seen the Grand Canyon can forget this unique scene.
6. A historic site in Atlanta shows visitors where Martin Luther King, Jr., lived and worked.
7. The Petrified Forest contains wood that water and dissolved minerals have changed into rock.
8. Every park offers whoever visits an opportunity to learn more about our country.